Stimmt! 1

Übungsheft A

Malcolm Pacey

ALWAYS LEARNING

PEARSON

1 Hallo! (Seiten 8–9)

1 Match the German to the correct meaning in English.

1 Tschüs, Christina.
2 Gut, danke. Und dir?
3 Wie geht's, Christina?
4 Hallo! Ich heiße Tobi. Wie heißt du?
5 Guten Tag! Ich heiße Christina.
6 Auf Wiedersehen, Tobi.
7 Nicht schlecht.

a Goodbye, Tobi.
b Hello! My name's Christina.
c Fine, thanks. And you?
d Hello! I'm called Tobi. What's your name?
e Not bad.
f Bye, Christina.
g How are you, Christina?

2 Write the dialogue from exercise 1 in the correct order.

Hallo! Ich heiße ______________________________

____

____

____

____

____

____

3 Look at the pictures and fill in the gaps in the conversations.

1 Hallo! Wie _ _ _ _ _ du?
Ich _ _ _ _ _ Roselyn.
Wie _ _ _ _'_, Roselyn?
_ _ _, danke.

2 Guten Tag! _ _ _ heißt du?
_ _ _ heiße Heather. Wie geht's?
Nicht _ _ _ _ _ _ _ _ _ . Und _ _ _?
Gut, _ _ _ _ _ .

Stefan Heather Tahir Roselyn

2 Eins, zwei, drei ... (Seiten 10–11)

1 **Find all the words for numbers 1 to 10 in German in the wordsearch. Write them out below as you find them. If you need help look at page 12.**

1 ____________ **6** ____________

2 ____________ **7** ____________

3 ____________ **8** ____________

4 ____________ **9** ____________

5 ____________ **10** ____________

z	w	e	i	k	n	a	s	v
p	h	u	d	s	d	r	e	i
b	l	a	f	o	e	g	k	e
s	e	c	h	s	r	d	m	r
p	i	h	t	n	z	e	h	n
f	j	t	e	g	n	i	l	f
ü	m	v	s	i	e	b	e	n
n	s	a	ü	r	u	h	ö	b
f	d	t	e	i	n	s	d	j

2 **Write each person's age in a full sentence in German. Unjumble the words in the cloud to find the missing numbers.**

Don't forget to write *Jahre* with a capital – it's a noun!

wlzöf *nnenuzeh* *shzneche* *lfe* *nzidehre* *ehffznün*

a

Ich bin elf Jahre alt.

____

b

____

____

c

____

____

d

____

____

e

____

____

f

____

____

3 Ich wohne in Deutschland (Seiten 12–13)

1 Complete the sentences to say where these people live. Then complete the question about you.

Ich ______________ in Berlin.

Sara ____________________________________

Peter ____________________________________

Matthias ____________________________________

Anuj ____________________________________

Wo ____________ ________?

Grammatik
ich wohne
du wohnst
er/sie wohnt

2 Complete the gaps with words from the cloud.

vierzehn Wales Jahre wohne Glasgow bin heiße ist alt

Guten Tag! Ich ______________ Philipp. Ich ______________ sechzehn ______________ alt. Ich ______________ in Aberystwyth. Das ist in ______________ .

Hallo! Ich heiße Lena. Ich bin ______________ Jahre ______________ . Ich wohne in ______________ . Das ______________ in Schottland.

3 Now write about yourself and where you live.

Hallo! Ich heiße ______________ . Ich ________ ______________ Jahre alt.

Ich ________ in ______________ . Das ________ in ______________ .

4 Meine Welt ist wunderbar! (Seiten 14–15)

1 **Write a sentence to describe each person.**

laut *freundlich* *intelligent* *musikalisch* *kreativ* *faul* *lustig* *sportlich*

1 
Ich bin ______________
____

2 
____
____

3 

____
____

4 
____
____

5 
____
____

6 
____
____

7 
____
____

8 
____
____

2 **Match each description to the picture of the person being described. Write the correct number in each box.**

1 Ich bin sehr laut und musikalisch.
2 Ich bin launisch, aber kreativ.
3 Ich bin freundlich und sehr intelligent.
4 Ich bin ziemlich faul, aber auch lustig.

Wer bin ich?

a 

Gregor ☐

b 
Marta ☐

c 
Pino ☐

d 
Ellie ☐

5 Meine Sachen (Seiten 16–17)

1 **Use the pictures and the words to write sentences about what you have.**

ich habe = I have

masculine	feminine	neuter
einen Computer	eine Gitarre	ein Handy
einen iPod	eine Wii	ein Keyboard
einen Fußball	eine Schlange	ein Skateboard

1  Ich habe einen Computer. ______________________

2  ______________________

3  ______________________

4 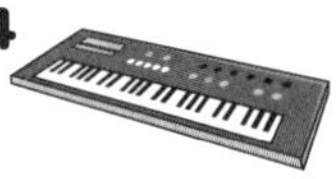 ______________________

5  ______________________

6  ______________________

7 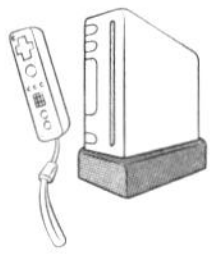 ______________________

8  ______________________

9  ______________________

2 **Write the correct question word to complete each question. Then translate the questions into English.**

wo = where, **wie** = how, **was** = what

In number 1, *wie* is translated as 'what', not 'how'.

1 Wie heißt du? What's your name?
2 ________ wohnst du? ______________________
3 ________ alt bist du? ______________________
4 ________ bist du? ______________________
5 ________ ist Hannover? ______________________
6 ________ ist deine Lieblingsmusik? ______________________

3 **Now write an answer to each question in exercise 2.**

Ich über mich (Seiten 18–19)

1 Find the six nouns in the cloud and write each of them with a capital letter. Then look up their gender in a dictionary and write in *der*, *die* or *das*.

fußballmannschaft lustig vogel wohne computer sehr musikalisch handy jahr heiße lieblingsauto

A noun is a person, place or thing. You write nouns with a capital letter in German. Always learn German nouns with their gender (masculine, feminine or neuter).

______________ ______________ ______________

______________ ______________ ______________

2 Write the phrases in German according to their gender.

die Musik
die Lieblingssache
das Spiel
das Lieblingswort
das T-Shirt
der Lieblingssport

Grammatik

Make sure you use the correct word for 'my' and 'your'. You need to know the gender of the noun to do this.

the	my	your
der Sport	mein Sport	dein Sport
die Musik	mein<u>e</u> Musik	dein<u>e</u> Musik
das Spiel	mein Spiel	dein Spiel

1 your music *deine* ______________
2 my game ______________
3 your T-shirt ______________
4 my favourite thing ______________
5 your favourite word ______________
6 your favourite sport ______________

3 Use the words in the cloud to complete the text.

auch aber einen habe heiße ist Lieblingsmonat meine sportlich vierzehn wohne

Hallo! Ich ______________ Max und ich bin ______________ Jahre alt. Ich ______________ in Kiel, in Deutschland, ______________ ich komme aus Swansea. Das ______________ in Wales. Ich bin ______________, lustig und ______________ sehr laut! Mein ______________ ist Dezember und ______________ Lieblingssendung ist „Die Simpsons". Ich ______________ ein iPad und auch ______________ Computer. Tschüs!

Wiederholung 1

1 Write the odd word out in each sentence.

1 Mein Lieblingssport ist **Handball** / **Fußball** / **Vogel**. ____________

2 Mein Lieblingsmonat ist **April** / **FIFA** / **Dezember**. ____________

3 Meine Lieblingsmusik ist **Pop** / **Rock** / **ein Porsche**. ____________

4 Meine Lieblingszahl ist **fünf** / **Australien** / **sieben**. ____________

5 Mein Lieblingsland ist **Rugby** / **Amerika** / **Deutschland**. ____________

2 Answer each question by writing a full sentence in German.

1 Was ist deine Lieblingssendung? „Eastenders"?

Nein, meine ... ____________

2 Was ist deine Lieblingsfußballmannschaft? Chelsea?

____

3 Was ist dein Lieblingsspiel? FIFA?

____

4 Was ist dein Lieblingssport? Tennis?

____

Grammatik

	a	**my**	**your**
masculine	ein	mein	dein
feminine	eine	meine	deine
neuter	ein	mein	dein

3 Choose words from the cloud to fill in the gaps.

nicht *Jahre* *Lieblingssport* *ziemlich* *wohne* *meine*
aber *freundlich* *Deutschland* *sportlich* *heiße* *habe*

Hallo! Ich ____________ Lina und ich ____________ in Walsrode. Das ist in ____________. Ich bin fünfzehn ____________ alt. Ich bin ____________ und ____________ intelligent, ____________ ich bin ____________ faul. Mein ____________ ist Hockey und ____________ Lieblingsmusik ist Pop. Ich ____________ einen Vogel aus Amerika. Er ist ____________ und sehr laut!

Wiederholung 2

1 Complete the table in English with information from the conversation.

Melanie: Hallo! Ich heiße Melanie. Wie heißt du?
Marco: Ich heiße Marco. Ich wohne in Straubing. Wo wohnst du?
Melanie: Ich wohne in Braunschweig und ich bin vierzehn Jahre alt. Wie alt bist du?
Marco: Ich bin zwölf Jahre alt. Wie bist du?
Melanie: Ich bin freundlich. Wie bist du?
Marco: Ich bin launisch.
Melanie: Hier ist meine Freundin. Sie heißt Jessie. Sie wohnt in Leipzig und ist dreizehn Jahre alt. Sie ist lustig.

Name	Town or city	Age	Character
Melanie			

2 Write about yourself and introduce a friend. Use exercise 1 as a model to help you.

If you need help with words, look at the vocabulary on pages 12 and 13.

Grammatik (Seiten 22–23)

1 Circle the correct verb form to complete each sentence.

1. Lukas **habe** / **hat** einen Computer.
2. Ich **hat** / **habe** einen Vogel zu Hause.
3. Wo **ist** / **bist** er?
4. Ich **ist** / **bin** musikalisch und auch sportlich.
5. Gloria **ist** / **bist** fünfzehn Jahre alt.
6. Wie alt **bist** / **bin** du?
7. Wo **hast** / **bin** ich?

Grammatik

ich bin	ich habe
du bist	du hast
er/sie/es ist	er/sie/es hat

2 Find nine verbs in the grid. Then write each one in the correct sentence.

r	e	s	w	o	h	n	s	t
i	b	e	l	h	k	a	p	r
a	h	ö	r	e	o	s	i	e
w	o	f	z	i	m	m	e	n
o	d	i	e	ß	m	w	b	k
h	ö	r	s	t	t	o	t	o
n	t	w	ö	n	p	h	o	m
t	e	p	r	k	v	n	u	m
g	s	h	e	i	ß	t	r	t

1. Ich _höre_ klassische Musik.
2. Erik __________ in Lübeck. Das ist in Deutschland.
3. __________ du gern Rockmusik?
4. Er __________ Michael.
5. __________ du Muhammad?
6. __________ du in der Schweiz?
7. Melissa __________ aus England und __________ in London.
8. Jenni __________ aus Dublin.

3 Write the verb forms next to the correct personal pronoun.

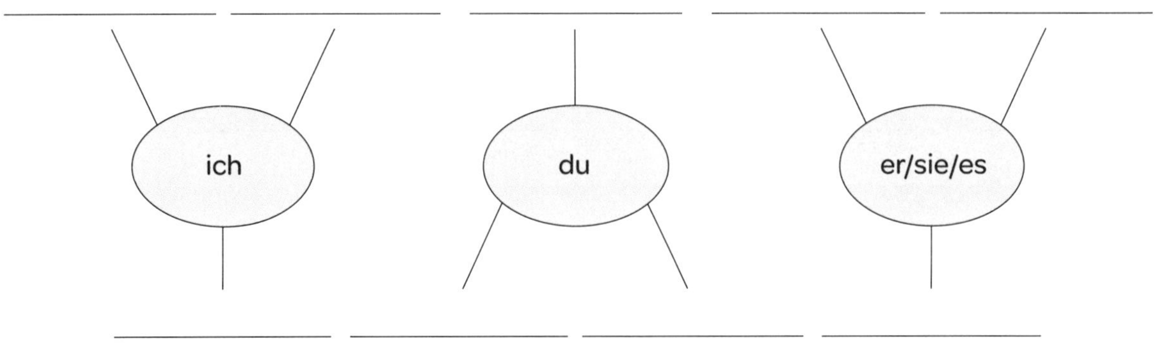

hast *bin* *wohnt* *bist* *hat* *habe* *wohne* *wohnst* *ist*

Mein Fortschritt

1 **Record your levels for *Kapitel* 1.**

2 **Look at the level descriptors on pages 59–60 and set your targets for *Kapitel* 2.**

3 **Fill in what you need to do to achieve these targets.**

Listening 	I have reached Level _____ in **Listening**. In *Kapitel* 2, I want to reach Level _____ I need to ______________________________ ______________________________ ______________________________ ______________________________
Speaking 	I have reached Level _____ in **Speaking**. In *Kapitel* 2, I want to reach Level _____ I need to ______________________________ ______________________________ ______________________________ ______________________________
Reading 	I have reached Level _____ in **Reading**. In *Kapitel* 2, I want to reach Level _____ I need to ______________________________ ______________________________ ______________________________ ______________________________
Writing 	I have reached Level _____ in **Writing**. In *Kapitel* 2, I want to reach Level _____ I need to ______________________________ ______________________________ ______________________________ ______________________________

Hallo! • Meeting and greeting

Wie heißt du?	*What's your name?*
Ich heiße ...	*My name is ...*
Hallo!	*Hello! / Hi!*
Guten Tag!	*Hello!*
Wie geht's?	*How are you?*
Gut, danke. Und dir?	*Fine, thanks. And you?*
Nicht schlecht.	*Not bad.*
Tschüs!	*Bye!*
Auf Wiedersehen!	*Goodbye!*

Die Zahlen 1–19 • Numbers 1–19

eins	*1*
zwei	*2*
drei	*3*
vier	*4*
fünf	*5*
sechs	*6*
sieben	*7*
acht	*8*
neun	*9*
zehn	*10*
elf	*11*
zwölf	*12*
dreizehn	*13*
vierzehn	*14*
fünfzehn	*15*
sechzehn	*16*
siebzehn	*17*
achtzehn	*18*
neunzehn	*19*
Wie alt bist du?	*How old are you?*
Ich bin ... Jahre alt.	*I am ... years old.*
Wie alt ist (Julia)?	*How old is (Julia)?*
(Julia) ist ... Jahre alt.	*(Julia) is ... years old.*

Wo wohnst du? • Where do you live?

Ich wohne in ...	*I live in ...*
Er/Sie/Es wohnt in ...	*He/She/It lives in ...*
... England	*England*
... Irland	*Ireland*
... Nordirland	*Northern Ireland*
... Schottland	*Scotland*
... Wales	*Wales*
... Deutschland	*Germany*
... Österreich	*Austria*
... der Schweiz	*Switzerland*

Wie bist du? • What are you like?

Ich bin ...	*I am ...*
Er/Sie ist ...	*He/She is ...*
faul	*lazy*
freundlich	*friendly*
intelligent	*intelligent*
kreativ	*creative*
launisch	*moody*
laut	*loud*
lustig	*funny*
musikalisch	*musical*
sportlich	*sporty*

Lieblingssachen • Favourite things

Mein Lieblingssport ist ...
My favourite sport is ...

Mein Lieblingsmonat ist ...
My favourite month is ...

Meine Lieblingsmusik ist ...
My favourite music is ...

Meine Lieblingszahl ist ...
My favourite number is ...

Meine Lieblingssendung ist ...
My favourite programme is ...

Meine Lieblingsfußballmannschaft ist ...
My favourite football team is ...

Mein Lieblingsspiel ist ...
My favourite game is ...

Mein Lieblingsland ist ...
My favourite country is ...

Mein Lieblingsauto ist ...
My favourite car is ...

Was ist dein Lieblingssport?
What's your favourite sport?

Was ist deine Lieblingszahl?
What's your favourite number?

Was ist dein Lieblingsland?
What's your favourite country?

Hast du einen Computer? • Have you got a computer?

Ich habe ...	*I have ...*
einen Computer	*a computer*
einen iPod	*an iPod*
einen Fußball	*a football*
eine Gitarre	*a guitar*
eine Wii	*a Wii*
eine Schlange	*a snake*
ein Handy	*a mobile phone*
ein Keyboard	*a keyboard*
ein Skateboard	*a skateboard*

Fragewörter • Question words

Wie?	*How?*
Was?	*What?*
Wo?	*Where?*
Woher?	*Where ... from?*
Wer?	*Who?*

Oft benutzte Wörter • High-frequency words

und	*and*
(und) auch	*(and) also*
aber	*but*
sehr	*very*
ziemlich	*quite*
nicht	*not*
Was denkst du?	*What do you think?*
Ich denke, ...	*I think ...*
Ich auch!	*Me too!*
Ich nicht!	*Not me!/That's not what I think!*
Was? Du spinnst!	*What? You're joking!*

1 Extreme Haustiere (Seiten 30–31)

1 **Write sentences to say what pets you have. Use the animals in the pictures.**

1 

2 

3 

4 

5 

6 

ein Meerschweinchen
einen Hamster
einen Goldfisch
eine Maus
~~*ein Pferd*~~
eine Schlange

1 Ich habe ein Pferd.
2 ______
3 ______
4 ______
5 ______
6 ______

2 **Read what these people say about their pets. Then complete the table in English.**

Ich habe eine Katze. Sie heißt Rosi und ist sehr launisch.

Amelie

Ich habe zwei Mäuse. Sie heißen Max und Moritz. Max ist total niedlich! Moritz ist ziemlich frech.

Mia

Wir haben zu Hause zwei Schlangen, Tibor und Magnus. Tibor ist sehr lang und Magnus ist schlank.

Erik

Wir haben ein Meerschweinchen. Es heißt Maik. Es ist dick und faul.

Philippa

Owner's name	Type of pet(s)	Name of pet(s)	Description
Amelie			
	mice		
		Tibor, Magnus	
			fat and

3 **Do you have a pet? Make one up if not! What is its name? What is it like?**

______

______

2 Supertiere (Seiten 32–33)

1 Write a sentence for each animal using the correct adjective from the cloud. Then translate the sentences into English.

intelligent
kräftig *superlustig*
faul *schnell*

er = he **sie** = she

1  Walter Wunderwellensittich

Er ist ______________________

He is ______________________

2  Marta Megamaus

____

____

3  Hermann Horrorhund

____

____

4  Sigi Superschlange

____

____

5  Harald Hamsterheld

____

____

2 Read the descriptions, then draw a picture to show what each animal can do.

1 Meine Schlange ist superintelligent! Sie kann lesen und Deutsch sprechen!

2 Mein Meerschweinchen ist sehr sportlich! Es kann Fußball spielen, Rad fahren und schnell laufen!

3 Mein Goldfisch ist lustig! Er kann singen und auch tanzen!

4 Mein Wellensittich ist cool. Er kann fliegen und Wii spielen.

3 Meine Familie (Seiten 34–35)

1 Read the numbers given as words and tick the correct lottery ball for each number.

a 65 ☐ 56 ☐ fünfundsechzig

b 27 ☐ 72 ☐ siebenundzwanzig

c 93 ☐ 39 ☐ neununddreißig

d 86 ☐ 68 ☐ sechsundachtzig

e 43 ☐ 34 ☐ vierunddreißig

f 67 ☐ 76 ☐ sechsundsiebzig

2 Complete the sentences about the families. You will need some words more than once.

einen Bruder *eine Schwester* *einen Vater*
zwei Brüder *zwei Schwestern* *eine Mutter*

Karlsruhe

1 Ich heiße Tom. Ich habe ________ ________. Ich habe auch ________ ________ und ________ ________. Ich wohne in ________.

Essen

2 Ich heiße Rishikesh. Es gibt fünf Personen in meiner Familie. Ich habe ________ ________, ________ ________ und auch ________ ________. Wir wohnen in ________.

Freiburg

3 Hallo! Ich heiße Markus. Ich habe ________ ________ und auch ________ ________. Meine Großeltern wohnen mit uns zusammen in ________.

3 Unjumble the bold words and rewrite the sentences. Write numbers as words.

1 Meine **rtetMu** ist [48] Jahre alt. ________________________

2 Ich habe [2] **deüBrr** und [1] **lbHaesrteschw**. ________________________

3 Meine **Sitefmutert** ist [52] Jahre alt. ________________________

Halbschwester = half-sister **Stiefmutter** = stepmother

4 Die Farben der Welt (Seiten 36–37)

1 **Complete the grid with the German words for the colours. Reveal the code word using the letters in the shaded boxes. It is a noun, so remember the capital letter!**

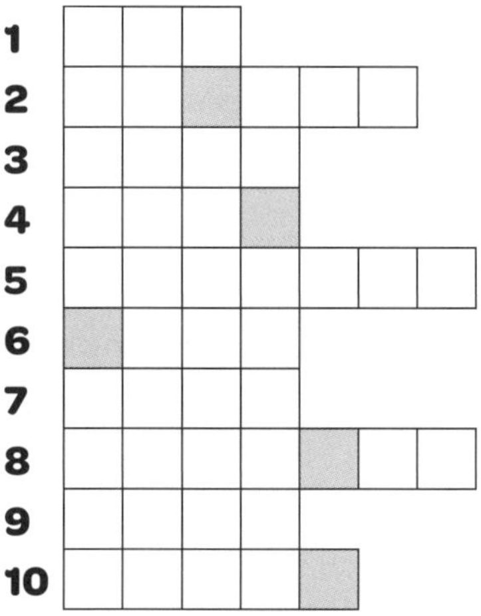

1 red
2 orange
3 green
4 blue
5 black
6 grey
7 white
8 purple
9 pink
10 brown

Markus hat hellblaue _ _ _ _ _ _.

2 **Complete the sentences with the correct form of the verb *haben* and the colour.**

When describing hair and eyes, you add an 'e' to the colours.

Grammatik

ich habe	wir haben
du hast	ihr habt
er/sie hat	sie/Sie haben

1 Ich ____________ kurze ____________ Haare.

2 Mein Bruder ____________ kurze ____________ Haare und ____________ Augen.

3 Meine Schwester ____________ mittellange ____________ Haare und ____________ Augen.

4 Mein Vater ____________ lange ____________ Haare.

5 Meine Mutter ____________ kurze ____________ Haare und hell ____________ Augen.

6 Meine Großeltern ____________ ____________ Haare und ____________ Augen.

5 Alles Gute! (Seiten 38–39)

1 Write the correct date in words next to each calendar page.

1 

am achten Mai ____________

2 

____

3 

____

4 

____

5 

____

6 

____

7 

____

am dritten Februar
am neunzehnten April
~~*am achten Mai*~~
am ersten Juni
am siebten September
am neunundzwanzigsten November
am zweiundzwanzigsten Dezember

2 Read the profiles and the statements below. Write 'true' or 'false' next to each statement.

Ich heiße Tim und ich wohne in Watford. Ich habe am dreiundzwanzigsten April Geburtstag. Mein Bruder Matthias hat auch im April Geburtstag, aber am dritten.

Hallo, hier ist Anna! Ich habe am vierten Juli Geburtstag. Das ist im Sommer – super! Meine Schwester Adele wohnt in Hamburg. Sie hat am 24. Dezember Geburtstag. Das findet sie nervig.

1 Tim and Matthias share the same birthday. ____________
2 Adele is 24 years old. ____________
3 Adele doesn't like her birthday. ____________
4 Matthias has his birthday before Tim. ____________
5 Anna's birthday is on 14 July. ____________
6 Anna likes her summer birthday. ____________

3 Write a short profile about yourself. Use the profiles in exercise 2 as models.

____

____

____

6 Eine Superfamilie (Seiten 40–41)

1 Draw a line to link each German question word to the correct English word.

Was?	Where ... from?
Wie?	Who?
Wo?	When?
Wer?	Where?
Wann?	How many ...?
Woher?	What?
Wie viele ...?	How?

You need to know the question words to understand what you're being asked. They're short and easy to learn!

2 Birgit Bauer, a celebrity, is being interviewed on Swiss television. Complete the script by using the information in the picture to answer the questions.

Spot the verb in each question. You will normally need the same verb in your answer.

Journalistin: **Birgit Bauer, willkommen!**

Birgit: Hallo Fleur!

Journalistin: **Also, Birgit, wie ist deine Familie?**

Birgit: Ich habe eine kleine Familie.

Journalistin: **Hast du Geschwister?**

Birgit: Ja, ich habe einen Bruder. Er ist ____________________.
Er kann ____________________ spielen.

Journalistin: **Toll. Und wie alt ist deine Mutter? Wann hat sie Geburtstag?**

Birgit: Meine Mutter ____________________
Sie ____________________

Journalistin: **Und wie ist dein Vater?**

Birgit: Mein Vater hat ____________________
und er ist ____________________

Journalistin: **Birgit, hast du Haustiere?**

Birgit: Ja, ich ____________________
____

Journalistin: **Wo wohnst du, Birgit?**

Birgit: ____________________

Journalistin: **Danke schön, Birgit! Tschüs!**

Wiederholung 1

1 **Find the adjectives eaten by *Susi Schlange* and write them on the lines below. Write the meaning in English next to each adjective.**

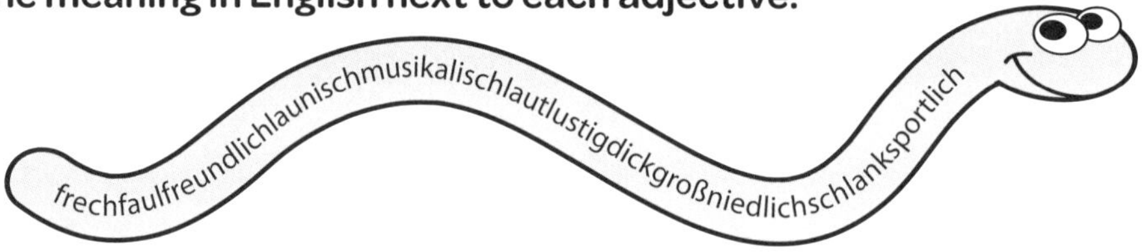

frech ____________ cheeky ____________ ____________ ____________

____________ ____________ ____________ ____________

____________ ____________ ____________ ____________

____________ ____________ ____________ ____________

____________ ____________ ____________ ____________

____________ ____________ ____________ ____________

2 **Translate these sentences into German. Use the adjectives from exercise 1.**

1 My father is lazy. ____________

2 My mother is creative and musical. ____________

3 My friend is fat but sporty. ____________

4 My sister is very slim. ____________

5 I am loud but quite cute. ____________

3 **Write sentences that include the plural form of each animal. Make sure you spell the numbers correctly!**

1  x2 Ich habe zwei Schlangen.

2  x3 ____________

3  x6 ____________

4  x4 ____________

5  x2 ____________

6  x5 ____________

Ich habe ...

 eine Schlange (-n)

 ein Kaninchen (-)

 eine Maus (Mäuse)

 einen Goldfisch (-e)

 eine Katze (-n)

 ein Pferd (-e)

Wiederholung 2

1 Write the house numbers as words.

Karl-Liebknecht-Straße 28 *achtund* ______________________

Grünewaldstraße 46 ______________________

Prinzstraße 67 ______________________

Willy-Brandt-Straße 73 ______________________

Neumannstraße 89 ______________________

2 Number the highlighted ants with the correct ordinal number. Use the tip box to remind you of how ordinal numbers are formed.

1st = erste 2nd = zweite 3rd = dritte 8th = achte
19th = neunzehnte 20th = zwanzigste

die Ameise = ant

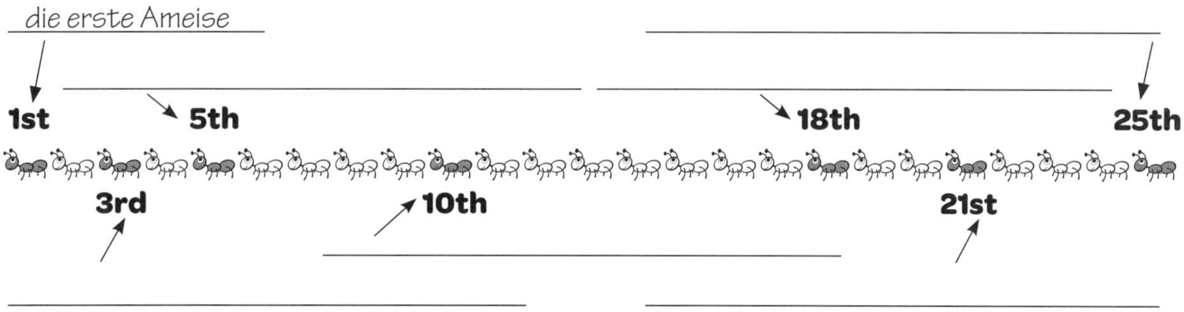

3 Use the code to write the words in German.

A	B	C	D	E	F	G	H	I	J	K	L	M	N	O
9	15	10	11	26	2	25	22	14	6	21	5	20	17	27

P	Q	R	S	T	U	V	W	X	Y	Z	Ä	Ö	Ü	ß
7	30	13	8	1	29	19	16	4	23	28	24	18	12	3

a 15 / 5 / 9 / 29 / 26 ______________

b 8 / 10 / 22 / 16 / 9 / 13 / 28 / 26 ______________

c 20 / 14 / 1 / 1 / 26 / 5 / 5 / 9 / 17 / 25 / 26 ______________

d 15 / 13 / 9 / 29 / 17 / 26 ______________

e 21 / 29 / 13 / 28 / 26 ______________

Use some of the decoded words to fill the gaps.

1 Marieke hat ______________ Augen.

2 Hast du ______________ ?

3 Sie hat ______________ und ______________ .

Grammatik (Seiten 44–45)

1 **Complete the verb table with the verbs from the cloud.**

	ich	du	er/sie/es	wir	ihr	Sie/sie
wohnen		wohnst			wohnt	wohnen
haben	habe		hat	haben		

hast *haben* *habt* *wohne* *wohnt* *wohnen*

2 **Use the correct verb forms in the table in exercise 1 to complete the sentences.**

1 Wir ______________ in Berlin.
2 Wo ______________ du?
3 ______________ Sie in Freiburg?
4 Ihr ______________ zwei Haustiere.
5 ______________ du einen Goldfisch?
6 Ich ______________ drei Geschwister.

du = 'you' to a friend or family member
ihr = 'you' to one or more friends or family members
Sie = 'you' in a polite way to any number of adults

3 **Use the correct verb form to complete each sentence.**

1 Ich ______________ neunzehn Jahre alt.
2 Du ______________ intelligent und lustig.
3 Er ______________ ganz freundlich.

bist
bin
ist

4 **Circle the correct word in each sentence. Then translate the sentences into English.**

1 Ich **kann / kannst** Fußball spielen.
2 Sie **kannst / kann** nicht schwimmen.
3 Er kann schnell **laufen / lauft**.
4 Du kannst gut **singt / singen**.
5 Ich **kannst / kann** Deutsch sprechen.

When you use a form of the verb *können*, like *kann* or *kannst*, there's always an infinitive at the end of the sentence.

5 **Translate the sentences into German. Use the sentences in exercises 2–4 to help you.**

1 We live in Cornwall.
2 You can play tennis.
3 They have three goldfish.
4 She is 14 years old.
5 He can swim well.
6 Are you 13 years old?
7 You [plural] have two sisters.
8 We live in Barnstaple.
9 Do they live in Salzburg?
10 I'm very moody.

Mein Fortschritt

1 Record your levels for *Kapitel* 2.

2 Look at the level descriptors on pages 59–60 and set your targets for *Kapitel* 3.

3 Fill in what you need to do to achieve these targets.

Listening 	I have reached Level ____ in **Listening**. In *Kapitel* 3, I want to reach Level ____ I need to ____________________
Speaking 	I have reached Level ____ in **Speaking**. In *Kapitel* 3, I want to reach Level ____ I need to ____________________
Reading 	I have reached Level ____ in **Reading**. In *Kapitel* 3, I want to reach Level ____ I need to ____________________
Writing 	I have reached Level ____ in **Writing**. In *Kapitel* 3, I want to reach Level ____ I need to ____________________

Haustiere • Pets

Hast du ein Haustier?	*Have you got a pet?*
Ich habe ...	*I have ...*
einen Goldfisch	*a goldfish*
einen Hamster	*a hamster*
einen Hund	*a dog*
ein Kaninchen	*a rabbit*
eine Katze	*a cat*
eine Maus	*a mouse*
ein Meerschweinchen	*a guinea pig*
ein Pferd	*a horse*
eine Schlange	*a snake*
einen Wellensittich	*a budgie*
kein Haustier	*no pet*

Eigenschaften • Qualities

Wie ist er/sie/es?	*What is he/she/ it like?*
Er/Sie/Es ist ...	*He/She/It is ...*
dick/schlank	*fat/thin*
frech/niedlich	*cheeky/cute*
gemein/süß	*mean/sweet*
groß/klein	*big/small*
kräftig	*strong*
schlau	*cunning*
(super)lustig	*(really) funny*
Er/Sie/Es kann ...	*He/She/It can ...*
Italienisch sprechen	*speak Italian*
fliegen	*fly*
Flöte/Fußball/Wii spielen	*play the flute/ football/on the Wii*
(schnell) laufen	*run (fast)*
lesen	*read*
Rad fahren	*ride a bike*
schwimmen	*swim*
singen	*sing*
springen	*jump*
tanzen	*dance*

Die Zahlen 20–100 • Numbers 20–100

zwanzig	*twenty*
dreißig	*thirty*
vierzig	*forty*
fünfzig	*fifty*
sechzig	*sixty*
siebzig	*seventy*
achtzig	*eighty*
neunzig	*ninety*
hundert	*hundred*
einundzwanzig	*twenty-one*
zweiundzwanzig	*twenty-two*

Meine Familie • My family

Es gibt ... Personen in meiner Familie.	*There are ... people in my family.*
meine Mutter	*my mother*
mein Vater	*my father*
mein Bruder	*my brother*
mein Stiefbruder/ Halbbruder	*my stepbrother/ half-brother*
meine Schwester	*my sister*
meine Stiefschwester/ Halbschwester	*my stepsister/ half-sister*
meine Eltern	*my parents*
meine Großeltern	*my grandparents*
Hast du Geschwister?	*Have you any brothers and sisters?*
Ich habe zwei Brüder.	*I have two brothers.*
Ich habe drei Schwestern.	*I have three sisters.*
Ich bin Einzelkind.	*I'm an only child.*
Ich habe keine Geschwister.	*I have no brothers and sisters.*

Die Farben • Colours

schwarz	*black*
weiß	*white*
grau	*grey*
braun	*brown*
rot	*red*
orange	*orange*
gelb	*yellow*
grün	*green*
blau	*blue*
indigoblau	*indigo*
violett	*violet*
lila	*purple*
rosa	*pink*
bunt	*brightly coloured*
hellblau/dunkelblau	*light blue/dark blue*

Haare und Augen • Hair and eyes

Er/Sie hat ...	*He/She has ...*
schwarze/braune/ blonde/rote Haare	*black/brown/ blond/red hair*
kurze/lange/ mittellange Haare	*short/long/ mid length hair*
blaue/braune/grüne/ graue Augen	*blue/brown/green/ grey eyes*

Die Monate • The months

Januar	*January*
Februar	*February*
März	*March*
April	*April*
Mai	*May*
Juni	*June*
Juli	*July*
August	*August*
September	*September*
Oktober	*October*
November	*November*
Dezember	*December*

Das Datum • The date

Wann hast du Geburtstag?	*When is your birthday?*
am 1. (ersten) Januar	*on 1 January*
am 3. (dritten) Februar	*on 3 February*
am 7. (siebten) März	*on 7 March*
am 8. (achten) April	*on 8 April*
am 15. (fünfzehnten) Mai	*on 15 May*
am 29. (neunund-zwanzigsten) Juni	*on 29 June*
Ich habe (heute) Geburtstag.	*It's my birthday (today).*

Oft benutzte Wörter • High-frequency words

und	*and*
aber	*but*
oder	*or*
ziemlich	*fairly, quite*
sehr	*very*

1 Bist du sportlich? (Seiten 54–55)

1 Write each sentence with the words in the correct order. Don't forget the full stop at the end of each sentence.

1 spiele Badminton Ich  *Ich spiele Badminton.*

2 Du Tischtennis spielst  ______

3 spielt Michelle Wasserball  ______

4 Fußball spielen Wir  ______

5 Ihr Basketball spielt  ______

6 Tennis und Steffi Matthias spielen  ______

2 Draw lines to match each phrase to the correct symbol.

sehr gern

gern

ziemlich gern

nicht gern

3 Write a sentence about each sport.

1   *Ich spiele sehr gern Tischtennis.*

2   ______

3   ______

4   ______

5   ______

6   ______

7   ______

2 Freizeit ist toll! (Seiten 56–57)

1 Use the words in the cloud to label each picture.

~~ich~~ fahre Rad ich spiele Gitarre ich ~~lese~~
ich schwimme ich mache Judo ich tanze

1  ich lese

2  ______

3  ______

4  ______

5  ______

6  ______

2 Find each German exchange student a good exchange partner in Wales by matching up people who have similar interests. Write the names of the Welsh pupils in the table below.

Schüler/Schülerinnen aus Deutschland	Schüler/Schülerinnen aus Wales
Ich spiele gern Gitarre. Musik ist mein Lieblingshobby. **Moritz S.**	Ich finde Sport cool. Ich spiele Tennis und auch Wasserball. **Glenys W.**
Ich bin sehr sportlich. Ich fahre Rad und auch Skateboard. **Ronni T.**	Meine Lieblingstiere sind Pferde! **Charlie J.**
Ich reite am Wochenende. Ich lese auch gern. **Sara H.**	Ich sehe gern fern. Das finde ich total super. „Man v Food" ist meine Lieblingssendung. **Heather B.**
Ich sehe gern Reality-Fernsehen. Ich lese auch gern. Ich finde Magazine toll. Ich fahre am Wochenende Rad. **Alida M.**	Ich schwimme und mache Judo. Ich finde Musik toll. **Dillon S.**

Moritz S.	Ronni T.	Sara H.	Alida M.

3 Read Anna's description of her sister Maria. Maria would like a German penfriend. Which person from exercise 2 would suit her best?

Meine Schwester, Maria, ist sehr freundlich. Sie sieht gern fern. Sie spielt nicht gern Gitarre. Das findet sie langweilig. Magazine liest sie sehr gern. Sie fährt gern Rad.

The best penfriend for Maria is: ______.

3 In meiner Freizeit (Seiten 58–59)

1 **Split up the words to make six sentences. Write each sentence in full.**

1 ichessepizzaoderhamburger

2 ichgeheindiestadt

3 ichhöremusik

4 ichgeheeinkaufen

5 ichgeheindenpark

6 ichmachesport

Be sure to begin all nouns with a capital letter.

1 ______________________

2 ______________________

3 ______________________

4 ______________________

5 ______________________

6 ______________________

2 **Draw lines to link each time phrase with its meaning.**

1 jeden Tag
2 dreimal pro Woche
3 am Wochenende
4 einmal pro Monat
5 viermal pro Monat
6 am Abend

a once a month
b three times a week
c every day
d at the weekend
e in the evening
f four times a month

3 **Rewrite the sentences from exercise 1, starting each one with a time phrase from exercise 2.**

Grammatik
After the time phrase, the verb goes in second place.
Ich spiele Xbox. → *Am Abend* ***spiele*** *ich Xbox.*

1 ______________________

2 ______________________

3 ______________________

4 ______________________

5 ______________________

6 ______________________

4 Ich bin online (Seiten 60–61)

1 Unscramble each sentence and write it on the line.

1 herunter lade Musik Ich ______________________

2 suche Internet Ich Infos im ______________________

3 YouTube Videos auf Wir sehen ______________________

4 Wir auf Facebook chatten ______________________

5 mit Ich Handy mache meinem Fotos ______________________

2 Match each English text message with the correct German sentence.

a

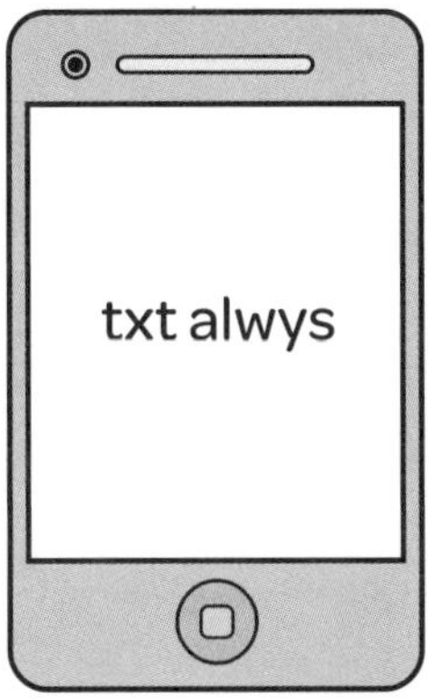

b

c

1 Ich simse immer. ☐

2 Ich spiele nie Computerspiele. ☐

3 Ich telefoniere manchmal mit Freunden. ☐

immer = always
manchmal = sometimes
nie = never

3 Translate into German these sentences about what people are going to do in the future.

morgen = tomorrow
am Montag = on Monday
am Wochenende = at the weekend
nächste Woche = next week
in zwei Wochen = in two weeks

1 We are going to make films next week.

Nächste Woche machen wir Filme.

2 On Monday I am going to search the internet.

____

3 Tomorrow you are going to chat on Facebook.

____

4 They are going to download some music in two weeks.

____

5 At the weekend Bronwyn is going to watch cat videos on YouTube.

____

1 Complete the email with the phrases from the cloud. Don't forget the punctuation!

1 ______________________

Danke 2 ______________________

3 ______________________ Es geht mir gut.

Ich habe viele Hobbys! Ich finde Sport super und ich spiele sehr gern Tischtennis, weil es toll ist! Ich gehe am Wochenende in den Park und spiele immer Fußball mit meinen Freunden. Musik finde ich toll. Ich höre jeden Tag Musik auf meinem iPhone und ich spiele Trompete. Meine Freundin Nerida spielt Keyboard in meiner Band. Manchmal essen wir zusammen einen Hamburger oder eine Pizza.

4 ______________________

5 ______________________

Andrea

für deine E-Mail!
Lieber Stephen,
Liebe Grüße
Wie geht's?
Schreib bald!

zusammen = together
Schreib bald! = Write soon!

2 Find the following features in the email above and underline them.

- 2 opinions
- 3 connecting words
- 2 time phrases
- 1 reference to another person
- 1 example of inverted word order (verb second after a time phrase)

Picking out features from a model text and adapting them will help you to add variety to your writing.

3 Complete the email below with the type of word indicated by the number.

Hallo Susi!

Ich heiße (1) Mona und ich komme aus Schottland. Ich ______________ (1) sehr gern Badminton, aber mein Lieblingssport ist ______________ (2). Ich ______________ (1) Badminton super. Ich lese auch ______________ (5) Magazine und ______________ (5) Blogs. Wasserball ______________ (4) Eishockey spiele ich nicht gern. Eishockey ist ______________. (3) Mein Freund Julian ______________ (1) auch gern ______________ (2), ______________ (4) nicht so gern Gitarre.

Deine Mona

Look at the model text in exercise 1 but try to use different words to fill the gaps.

(1) verb
(2) noun
(3) adjective
(4) connecting word
(5) frequency expression

Wiederholung 1

1 Fill in the missing adjectives in the right places in the diagram.

positive **neutral** **negative**

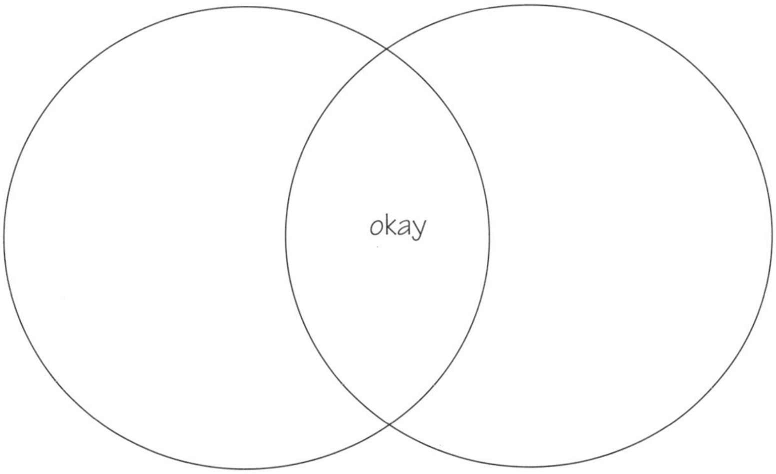

~~okay~~
stinklangweilig
toll
irre
furchtbar
cool
super
nicht schlecht
langweilig
gut
nervig

2 Do you like these activities? Use some of the adjectives from exercise 1.

1 

Ich schwimme gern. ______

Ich finde es ______

2 

Ich tanze ______

Ich ______

3 

Ich esse ______ Pizza.

Ich ______

4 

Ich spiele ______

Ich ______

3 Read the online interview. Write each activity, in German, in the table.

Susi: Was macht ihr gern am Computer?
Mareike: Ich spiele sehr gern Computerspiele, aber ich suche nicht gern Infos im Internet.
Abdul: Ich sehe sehr gern Videos auf YouTube! Ich chatte auch ziemlich gern mit Freunden auf Facebook.
Liesel: Ich simse gern und lade ziemlich gern Musik herunter.

Mareike	Computerspiele			Internet
Abdul				
Liesel				

Wiederholung 2

1 **Read the dialogue and then complete the table in English. Write the activities that Simmi and Adele are doing in the future.**

Simmi: Hey, du! Wie geht's?
Adele: Mir geht's super. Und dir?
Simmi: Danke, gut! Was machst du?
Adele: Ich chatte mit Lukas auf Facebook.
Simmi: Spielst du am Montag Fußball?
Adele: Ja, klar! Ich spiele immer am Montag Fußball mit Suzanne.
Simmi: Kannst du am Wochenende Tennis spielen?
Adele: Am Wochenende gehe ich schwimmen.
Simmi: Kannst du nächste Woche in den Park kommen?
Adele: Ja! Wir gehen nächste Woche zusammen in den Park.
Simmi: Toll! Dann gehe ich am Montag einkaufen und am Wochenende gehe ich ins Kino.

	now	at the weekend	on Monday	next week
Simmi				
Adele	*chat on Facebook*			

2 **Write an email to your penfriend saying what you like doing on the computer and what you are going to do at the weekend.**

Ich chatte mit Freunden auf Facebook.
Ich mache Fotos oder Filme.
Ich suche Infos im Internet.
Ich simse.
Ich lade Musik herunter.
Ich sehe Videos.
Ich surfe im Internet.
Ich spiele Computerspiele
Ich telefoniere mit Freunden.

Use these time phrases to help you write about what you are going to do in the future.

morgen = tomorrow
am Montag = on Monday
nächste Woche = next week
in zwei Wochen = in two weeks

Don't forget, you can write about 'we' using *wir* and the correct form of the verb.

Grammatik (Seiten 68–69)

1 Choose the correct form of the regular verb from the cloud to complete each sentence. Be careful as there are more verbs than you need!

1 Wir ______________ zweimal pro Woche Fußball.
2 Ich ______________ am Wochenende in der Disko.
3 ______________ du auch Wasserball?
4 Herr Wallender ______________ mit Freunden Tennis.
5 Er ______________ einmal pro Woche in den Park.
6 Mona und Lili ______________ am Sonntag einkaufen.
7 ______________ er immer Musik?
8 ______________ du am Freitag Judo?

spielen *tanzt*
hört *spielst*
geht *gehen*
spielt *tanze*
machst *schwimmt*

2 Fill in the gaps with the correct form of the irregular verb.

1 Er ______________ oft fern. Seine Lieblingssendung ______________ „Deutschland sucht den Superstar".
2 ______________ du am Montag Rad?
3 Ich ______________ sehr gern Magazine.
4 ______________ du gern Musikvideos?
5 Frau Escher ______________ gern Skateboard.
6 Paul ______________ gern Comics.

liest
fährst
siehst
sieht
fährt
lese
ist

3 Write five sentences by choosing an item from each column. Then translate your sentences into English.

Example: Ich spiele morgen Computerspiele.
I am going to play computer games tomorrow.

Ich	fahre	am Wochenende	Musik.
	spiele	jeden Tag	Judo.
	mache	dreimal pro Woche	Rad.
	gehe	jeden Abend	ins Kino.
	höre	nächste Woche	Pizza und Schokolade.
	esse	morgen	Computerspiele.

Mein Fortschritt

1 Record your levels for *Kapitel* 3.

2 Look at the level descriptors on pages 59–60 and set your targets for *Kapitel* 4.

3 Fill in what you need to do to achieve these targets.

Listening 	I have reached Level _____ in **Listening**. In *Kapitel* 4, I want to reach Level _____ I need to ______________________________ ______________________________ ______________________________ ______________________________
Speaking 	I have reached Level _____ in **Speaking**. In *Kapitel* 4, I want to reach Level _____ I need to ______________________________ ______________________________ ______________________________ ______________________________
Reading 	I have reached Level _____ in **Reading**. In *Kapitel* 4, I want to reach Level _____ I need to ______________________________ ______________________________ ______________________________ ______________________________
Writing 	I have reached Level _____ in **Writing**. In *Kapitel* 4, I want to reach Level _____ I need to ______________________________ ______________________________ ______________________________ ______________________________

Wörter

Bist du sportlich? • Are you sporty?

Ich bin (sehr/ziemlich/ nicht sehr) sportlich.	*I am (very/quite/ not very) sporty.*
Was spielst du?	*What do you play?*
Ich spiele ...	*I play ...*
Ich spiele gern ...	*I like playing ...*
Ich spiele ziemlich gern ...	*I quite like playing ...*
Ich spiele nicht gern ...	*I don't like playing ... playing ...*
Badminton	*badminton*
Basketball	*basketball*
Eishockey	*ice hockey*
Fußball	*football*
Handball	*handball*
Tennis	*tennis*
Tischtennis	*table tennis*
Volleyball	*volleyball*
Wasserball	*water polo*

Was machst du gern? • What do you like doing?

Was machst du gern?	*What do you like doing?*
Ich fahre Rad.	*I ride my bike.*
Ich fahre Skateboard.	*I go skateboarding.*
Ich fahre Ski.	*I ski.*
Ich fahre Snowboard.	*I snowboard.*
Ich lese.	*I read.*
Ich mache Judo.	*I do judo.*
Ich mache Karate.	*I do karate.*
Ich reite.	*I go horse riding.*
Ich schwimme.	*I swim.*
Ich sehe fern.	*I watch TV.*
Ich spiele Gitarre.	*I play the guitar.*
Ich tanze.	*I dance.*

Wie findest du das? • What do you think of it?

Ich finde es ...	*I think it's ...*
Es ist ...	*It's ...*
irre	*amazing*
super	*super*
toll	*great*
cool	*cool*
gut	*good*
nicht schlecht	*not bad*
okay	*okay*
langweilig	*boring*
nervig	*annoying*
stinklangweilig	*deadly boring*
furchtbar	*awful*

Was machst du in deiner Freizeit? • What do you do in your free time?

Ich chille.	*I chill out.*
Ich esse Pizza oder Hamburger.	*I eat pizza or hamburgers.*
Ich gehe einkaufen.	*I go shopping.*
Ich gehe ins Kino.	*I go to the cinema.*
Ich gehe in den Park.	*I go to the park.*
Ich gehe in die Stadt.	*I go into town.*
Ich höre Musik.	*I listen to music.*
Ich mache Sport.	*I do sport.*
Ich spiele Xbox oder Wii.	*I play Xbox or on the Wii.*

Ich bin online • I'm online

Was machst du am Computer?	*What do you do on the computer?*
Was machst du auf deinem Handy?	*What do you do on your mobile?*
Ich chatte mit Freunden auf Facebook.	*I chat with friends on Facebook.*
Ich lade Musik herunter.	*I download music.*
Ich mache Fotos oder Filme.	*I take photos or make films.*
Ich sehe Videos.	*I watch videos.*
Ich simse.	*I text.*
Ich spiele Computerspiele.	*I play computer games.*
Ich suche und lese Infos für die Hausaufgaben.	*I look for and read information for my homework.*
Ich surfe im Internet.	*I surf the internet.*
Ich telefoniere mit Freunden.	*I call my friends.*
Ich mache ziemlich viel auf meinem Handy.	*I do quite a lot of things on my mobile.*

Oft benutzte Wörter • High-frequency words

Wie oft?	*How often?*
(sehr/ziemlich/nicht so) oft	*(very/quite/not so) often*
einmal/zweimal/dreimal pro Woche/pro Monat	*once/twice/three times a week/a month*
jeden Tag	*every day*
jeden Morgen	*every morning*
manchmal	*sometimes*
immer	*always*
nie	*never*
Wann?	*When?*
am Wochenende	*at the weekend*
am Abend	*in the evening*
heute	*today*
morgen	*tomorrow*
am Montag	*on Monday*
nächste Woche	*next week*
in zwei Wochen	*in two weeks*

1 Ich mag Deutsch! (Seiten 76–77)

1 **Label the exercise books with the correct school subjects.**

1 
____

2 
____

3 
____

4 
____

5 
____

6 
____

7 
____

8 
____

Deutsch *Erdkunde* *Geschichte* *Informatik* *Kunst*
Naturwissenschaften *Technik* *Theater*

2 **Draw lines to match the symbols with the phrases.**

1  **2**  **3**  **4**  **5** 

a ich liebe **b** ich hasse **c** ich mag **d** ich mag [...] sehr **e** ich mag [...] nicht

3 **Circle the correct adjective in each sentence.**

1 Ich hasse Technik, weil es **toll / nutzlos** ist.
2 Mein Lieblingsfach ist Kunst, weil es **interessant / schwierig** ist.
3 Ich mag Englisch sehr, weil Englisch **nützlich / langweilig** ist.
4 Ich liebe Mathe, weil es **furchtbar / einfach** ist.
5 Ich mag Geschichte nicht, weil es **langweilig / interessant** ist.
6 Ich mag Erdkunde, weil es **nicht schwierig / furchtbar** ist.

toll

furchtbar

nutzlos

nützlich

schwierig

einfach

interessant

langweilig

2 Was und wann? (Seiten 78–79)

1 **Write the times in numbers on the clocks. Write the times in order, starting with the earliest time on the first clock.**

Es ist .... Uhr. = It is ... o'clock.

Es ist fünf Uhr vierzig.
Es ist sieben Uhr zwanzig.
Es ist zwanzig Uhr siebzehn.
Es ist neun Uhr dreiundvierzig.
Es ist dreizehn Uhr fünfundzwanzig.
Es ist neunzehn Uhr dreißig.

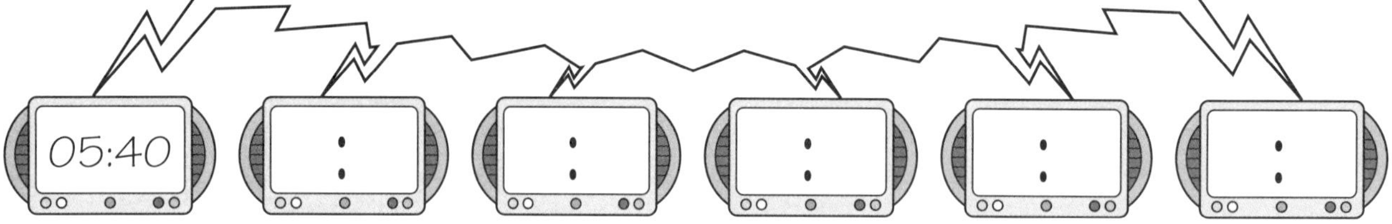

2 **Look at the timetable and write 'true' or 'false' next to each statement.**

Montag	Dienstag	Mittwoch	Donnerstag	Freitag
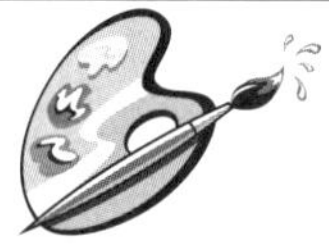				

die Doppelstunde = double period

1. Am Mittwoch habe ich Deutsch. ______
2. Am Freitag habe ich Musik. ______
3. Ich habe am Montag Kunst und Informatik. ______
4. Theater ist am Mittwoch und Donnerstag. ______
5. Am Freitag habe ich keine Schule. ______
6. Am Dienstag habe ich eine Doppelstunde Mathe. ______

3 **Write a sentence saying when you have each lesson.**

1.  Am Montag habe ich ______
2.  Am Mittwoch und Freitag ______
3.  Am Dienstag ______
4.  Am Mittwoch und Donnerstag ______

3 Lehrer und Lehrerinnen (Seiten 80–81)

1 Unscramble the words in bold and rewrite each sentence correctly. Then translate the sentences into English.

freundlich *streng* *launisch* *unpünktlich* *nervig* *lustig*

1 Meine Deutschlehrerin ist sehr **stliug**. ______________________

____

2 Mein Sportlehrer ist ziemlich **phücntklinu**. ______________________

____

3 Ich finde meine Geschichtslehrerin zu **egsntr**. ______________________

____

4 Der Mathelehrer ist ein bisschen **vriegn**. ______________________

____

5 Frau Daler finde ich zu **nscauihl**. ______________________

____

6 Ist dein Kunstlehrer sehr **rldinucehf**? ______________________

____

2 a Choose the correct possessive pronouns in the text about Tobias.
b Write a paragraph about Emilie using the picture and text (a) to help you.

Grammatik
sein = his **ihr** = her
Sein and *ihr* have to agree with the noun they are used with.
For feminine nouns, add an 'e'. For example:
seine Lieblingsmusik = his favourite music
ihre Lieblingsmusik = her favourite music

a Emilie hat einen Bruder. Er heißt Tobias.
Seine / Ihre Lieblingssendung ist „Ich bin ein Star!"
Sein / Ihr Lieblingssport ist Schwimmen und
sein / ihr Lieblingsfach in der Schule ist Englisch.

b Tobias hat eine Schwester. Sie heißt Emilie.

____

____

____

4 Im Klassenzimmer (Seiten 82–83)

1 Use the words in the cloud to label the items in the classroom.

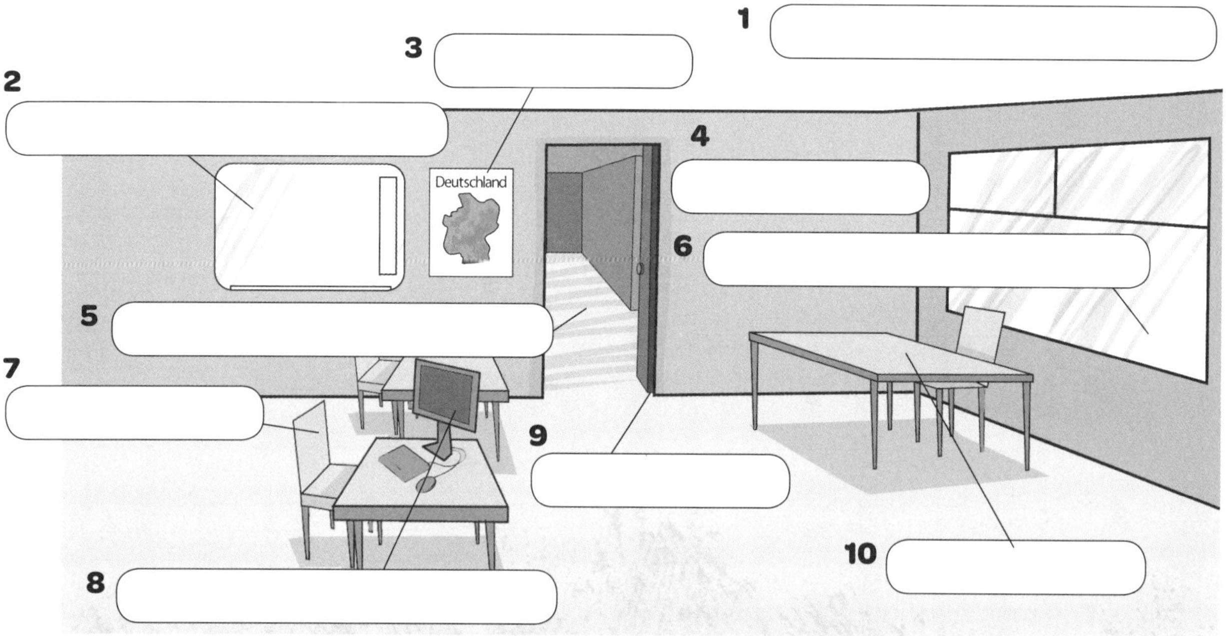

das Klassenzimmer   der Computer   das Fenster   der Korridor   das Poster
der Stuhl   der Tisch   die Tür   die Wand   das Whiteboard

2 Draw lines to match each German phrase with the correct English meaning.

1 neben dem Computer
2 im Klassenzimmer
3 an der Wand
4 neben der Tür
5 im Korridor

a on the wall
b next to the computer
c in the corridor
d in the classroom
e next to the door

3 Use the phrases in exercise 2 to help you answer the questions.

1 Wo ist Herr Peters? Herr Peters ist ____________________

2 Wo sind die Poster? ____________________

3 Wo ist das Whiteboard? ____________________

4 Wo ist das Buch? ____________________

5 Wo sind die Stühle? ____________________

Mein Lieblingstag (Seiten 84–85)

1 Henry is staying with a host family in Germany. Skim read the email he has written to his class in Dublin and find five words you don't know. Write each one in the table, look up its meanings in a dictionary and add what type of word it is.

German	English	Type of word (noun, verb, adjective, etc.)

Liebe Klasse 10b,
Lieber Herr Flynn,

Hallo aus Lübeck in Norddeutschland!

Meine Gastfamilie ist sehr freundlich. Der Sohn heißt Michael und ist 15 Jahre alt. Wir sind beide zusammen in Klasse 10. Die Tochter, Valentina, ist 18 Jahre alt. Valentina ist in der 12. Klasse.

In der Schule lerne ich Englisch, Französisch, Mathe, Musik, Naturwissenschaften und auch Kunst und Technik. Mein Lieblingsfach ist natürlich Englisch und ich hasse Musik. Musik haben wir zweimal pro Woche. Der Lehrer ist immer unpünktlich und launisch. Ich mag Englisch, weil es einfach ist!

Die Schulregeln sind ziemlich locker. Man darf Handys auf dem Schulhof benutzen, aber nicht im Klassenzimmer. Man darf auch Jeans und ein T-Shirt in der Schule tragen!

Schreib bald.

Liebe Grüße,

Henry

With a word you don't know, ask youself:
- Is it similar to an English word or to a word I already know?
- Can I work out the meaning from the context?

If not, look up its meaning in a dictionary.

2 Read Henry's email again and answer the questions in English.

1 Where is Lübeck? ____________
2 Who is Michael? ____________
3 What class is Henry in at school in Germany? ____________
4 How often does Henry have music? ____________
5 Who is not on time? ____________
6 What is Henry's favourite subject? ____________
7 Where can't you use mobiles? ____________

Before reading a text, read the questions to help you to focus on what you are reading. You probably don't need to understand every word to answer the questions.

Wiederholung 1

1 Read the text and complete the timetable in German.

In der ersten Stunde haben wir Geschichte.
Nach der Pause haben wir Deutsch.
In der sechsten Stunde haben wir Naturwissenschaften.
Mein Lieblingsfach haben wir nach der Mittagspause, Englisch.
Ich finde Sport langweilig. Das ist in der vierten Stunde.
Ich habe Erdkunde vor der Pause.

vor der Pause = before break
nach der Mittagspause = after lunch break

09:05	1. Stunde	*Geschichte*
09:50	2. Stunde	
10:35	Pause	
10:50	3. Stunde	
11:35	4. Stunde	
12:20	Mittagspause	
13:30	5. Stunde	
14:15	6. Stunde	

2 Look at the timetable in exercise 1 and write the time in words when each lesson starts.

1 Ich habe Geschichte um *neun Uhr fünf.*
2 Ich habe ________________ um ________________
3 ________________
4 ________________
5 ________________
6 ________________

**3 Separate the words in the shapes to make sentences.
Then circle the infinitive verb in each sentence and underline the part of *dürfen*.**

1 IchdarfinderPauseamComputerspielen.

2 MandarfheuteHandballspielen.

3 DudarfstnichtaufdemTischsitzen.

4 MandarfkeineHandysbenutzen.

Grammatik
The verb *dürfen* tells you what you're allowed to do. It is used with an infinitive at the end of the sentence, just like *können*.

Wiederholung 2

1 Write something nice about four of your teachers! Use the adjectives below to help you write about each of them.

Example: Meine Sportlehrerin heißt Frau Mann. Sie ist sehr sportlich und lustig!

freundlich *fair* *jung* *lustig* *intelligent* *sportlich* *pünktlich*

Make your sentence more interesting with qualifiers like *sehr, ziemlich, ein bisschen.* To make your sentence longer, use connectives like *und, oder, aber.*

1 ______________________________

2 ______________________________

3 ______________________________

4 ______________________________

2 Rearrange each sentence so that all the words are in the right order.

Grammatik

Remember that *weil* is so *vile* that it pushes the verb to the end of the sentence!

Extra hint:

Always put a comma **before** *weil*!

1 gern lerne Mathe Ich weil nützlich sehr ist es

____

2 machen Sport Wir super es weil ist

____

3 Ich Englisch liebe weil Lehrer ist der lustig

____

4 Frau Volleyball Wörth spielt sie ist weil sportlich

____

3 Write two sentences about subjects or teachers you like at school. Give your reason, using *weil*.

1 ______________________________

2 ______________________________

Grammatik (Seiten 90–91)

1 **Circle the correct word in bold in each sentence. There's only one correct answer!**

masculine	feminine	neuter
Computer	Gitarre	Whiteboard
Stuhl	Tür	Poster

Grammatik

Remember that after *es gibt* the word for 'a' changes to *einen* for masculine nouns. For example, *ein Computer* → *Es gibt* ***einen*** *Computer im Klassenzimmer.*

There is no change for feminine or neuter nouns.

1 Es gibt **einen / eine / ein** Computer im Klassenzimmer. (einen circled)
2 Auf dem Tisch gibt es **einen / eine / ein** Gitarre.
3 Es gibt **einen / eine / ein** Whiteboard im Klassenzimmer.
4 Im Korridor gibt es **einen / eine / ein** Stuhl.
5 Im Klassenzimmer gibt es **einen / eine / ein** Tür.
6 Es gibt **einen / eine / ein** Poster an der Wand.

2 **Circle the correct possessive pronoun in bold. Then translate the sentences into English.**

If you've forgotten the gender, check in a dictionary or vocabulary list.

1 **Sein / Seine** Deutschlehrer kommt aus der Schweiz.

____

2 **Ihr / Ihre** Lieblingsfach ist Geschichte.

____

3 Frau Schmidt ist Schulleiterin. **Ihr / Ihre** Schule ist 90 Jahre alt.

____

die Schulleiterin = headmistress

4 Herr Bauer ist cool. **Sein / Seine** Pferd ist sehr groß.

____

3 **Rewrite the sentences, starting with your choice of time phrase from the cloud. Remember to change the word order so the verb comes second.**

heute *morgen* *am Montag* *nach der Pause* *in der vierten Stunde*

1 Wir haben Deutsch. Heute haben wir Deutsch.
2 Ich habe Sport. ______________________________
3 Wir haben Mathe. ______________________________
4 Du hast Geschichte. ______________________________
5 Ich habe Erdkunde. ______________________________

Mein Fortschritt

1 **Record your levels for *Kapitel* 4.**

2 **Look at the level descriptors on pages 59–60 and set your targets for *Kapitel* 5.**

3 **Fill in what you need to do to achieve these targets.**

Listening 	I have reached Level ______ in **Listening**. In *Kapitel* 5, I want to reach Level ______ I need to ____ ____ ____ ____
Speaking 	I have reached Level ______ in **Speaking**. In *Kapitel* 5, I want to reach Level ______ I need to ____ ____ ____ ____
Reading 	I have reached Level ______ in **Reading**. In *Kapitel* 5, I want to reach Level ______ I need to ____ ____ ____ ____
Writing 	I have reached Level ______ in **Writing**. In *Kapitel* 5, I want to reach Level ______ I need to ____ ____ ____ ____

Schulfächer • School subjects

Deutsch	*German*
Englisch	*English*
Erdkunde	*geography*
Geschichte	*history*
Informatik	*ICT*
Kunst	*art*
Mathe	*maths*
Musik	*music*
Naturwissenschaften	*science*
Sport	*sport, PE*
Technik	*technology*
Theater	*drama*

Meinungen • Opinions

mein Lieblingsfach ist ...	*my favourite subject is ...*
ich mag ... (sehr)	*I like ... (a lot)*
ich liebe	*I love*
ich mag ... nicht	*I don't like ...*
ich hasse	*I hate*
gut	*good*
toll	*great*
furchtbar	*awful*
einfach	*easy*
schwierig	*difficult*
interessant	*interesting*
langweilig	*boring*
nützlich	*useful*
nutzlos	*useless*
faszinierend	*fascinating*
nervig	*irritating*
supercool	*really cool*
stinklangweilig	*dead boring*

Die Wochentage • The days of the week

Montag (Mo.)	*Monday*
Dienstag (Di.)	*Tuesday*
Mittwoch (Mi.)	*Wednesday*
Donnerstag (Do.)	*Thursday*
Freitag (Fr.)	*Friday*
Samstag (Sa.)	*Saturday*
Sonntag (So.)	*Sunday*
Was hast du am Montag?	*What do you have on Monday?*
Am Dienstag habe ich ...	*I have ... on Tuesday*
Am Sonntag haben wir keine Schule.	*We have no school on Sunday.*

Die Zeit • Time

Wann?	*When?*
Um wie viel Uhr?	*At what time?*
Um 8:30 Uhr (acht Uhr dreißig).	*At 8:30.*
Wie viel Uhr ist es?	*What time is it?*
Es ist 9:50 Uhr (neun Uhr fünfzig).	*It's 9:50.*
in der ersten Stunde	*in the first lesson*
vor der Pause	*before break*
nach der Mittagspause	*after the lunch break*

Eigenschaften • Characteristics

Er/Sie ist ...	*He/She is ...*
alt	*old*
fair	*fair*
freundlich	*friendly*
jung	*young*
launisch	*moody*
lustig	*funny*
nervig	*annoying*
streng	*strict*
unpünktlich	*unpunctual*

In der Schule • In school

die Lehrerin(-nen)	*teacher (female)*
die Deutsch-lehrerin(-nen)	*German teacher (female)*
der Lehrer(–)	*teacher (male)*
der Sportlehrer(–)	*sports teacher (male)*
Was gibt es?	*What is there?*
Es gibt einen/eine/ein ...	*There is a ...*
Es gibt viele ...	*There are lots of ...*
das Klassenzimmer(–)	*classroom*
der Tisch(-e)	*table*
der Stuhl(¨-e)	*chair*
der Computer(–)	*computer*
das Whiteboard(-s)	*whiteboard*
das Poster(–)	*poster*
das Fenster(–)	*window*
die Wand(¨-e)	*wall*
die Tür(-en)	*door*
der Korridor(-e)	*corridor*

Wo ist das? • Where is it?

in der Schule	*in the school*
im Klassenzimmer	*in the classroom*
im Korridor	*in the corridor*
an der Wand	*on the wall*
am Fenster	*by the window*
am Tisch	*at the table*
auf dem Tisch	*on the table*
neben der Tür	*near/next to the door*

Oft benutzte Wörter • High-frequency words

weil	*because*
sein/seine	*his*
ihr/ihre	*her*
zu	*too*
sehr	*very*
ziemlich	*quite, fairly*
ein bisschen	*a bit*
nicht	*not*
haben	*to have*
sein	*to be*
in	*in*
an	*at, by, on (wall)*
auf	*on (top of)*
neben	*near, next to*
heute	*today*
morgen	*tomorrow*
vor	*before*
nach	*after*

1 **Match each sentence to the correct set of pictures.**

1 Es gibt keinen Bahnhof, aber es gibt ein Schwimmbad.
2 Es gibt keine Kegelbahn, aber es gibt ein Schloss.
3 Es gibt keine Imbissstube, aber es gibt einen Bahnhof.
4 Es gibt kein Kino, aber es gibt einen Bahnhof.
5 Es gibt keine Kirche, aber es gibt ein Kino.
6 Es gibt keinen Park, aber es gibt einen Marktplatz.

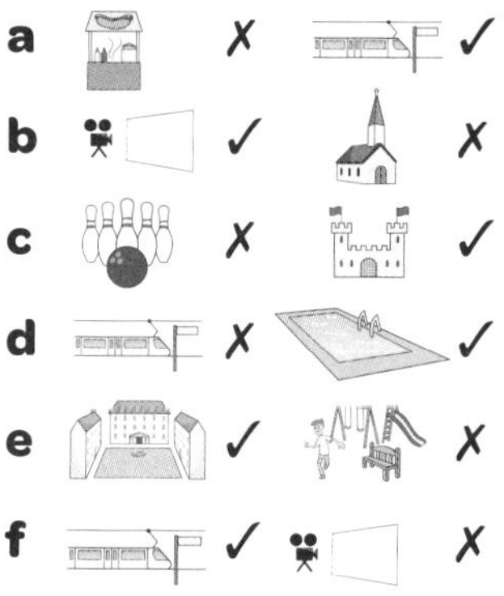

2 **Use the information in the pictures to write sentences like those in exercise 1.**

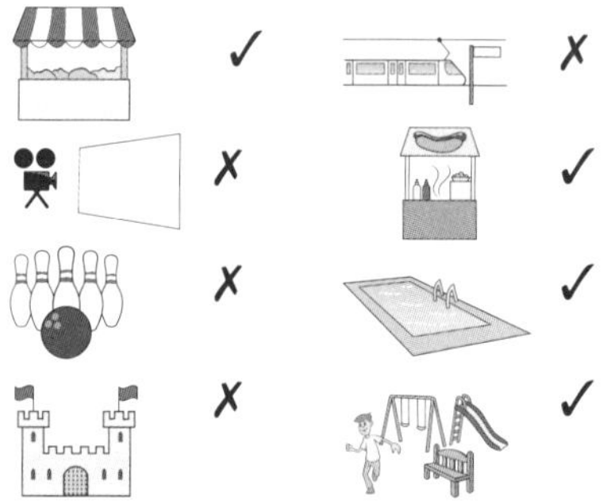

1 Es gibt keinen ______________________
2 ______________________
3 ______________________
4 ______________________

3 **Read the German tourist website for Bridport in Dorset. Put ticks and crosses in the table to show what there is and isn't in Bridport.**

Bridport in Dorset, England

Bridport ist eine tolle Stadt für Touristen aus Deutschland. Es gibt eine Touristeninformation am Marktplatz. Es gibt am Wochenende einen Markt auf dem Marktplatz und hier kann man einkaufen gehen. Es gibt auch eine Imbissstube auf dem Marktplatz. Man kann in Bridport Tennis und Fußball spielen, aber es gibt kein Schwimmbad und keine Kegelbahn. Man kann auch in den Park gehen. Es gibt hier ein Theater und auch ein Kino. Es gibt auch drei Kirchen in Bridport. Es gibt hier keinen Bahnhof.

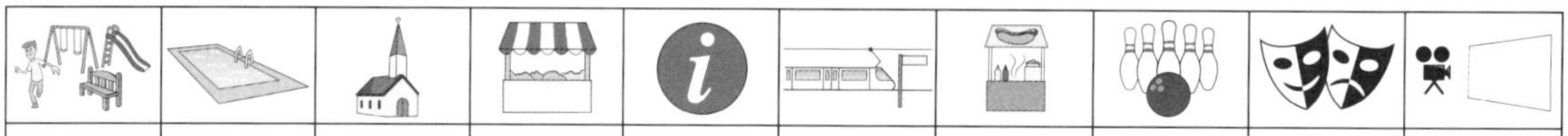

2 Wir gehen einkaufen! (Seiten 100–101)

1 Read the prices of the souvenirs. Write each price in numbers under the souvenir.

das Freundschaftsband – vier Euro fünfundneunzig
die Postkarte – fünfundsiebzig Cent
der Kuli – achtzig Cent
der Aufkleber – ein Euro zwanzig
das Kuscheltier – dreizehn Euro achtzig
die Kappe – achtunddreißig Euro sechzig
der Schlüsselanhänger – sechs Euro vierzig

Prices are written like this:
€1 = *ein Euro*
€1,50 = *ein Euro fünfzig*
€0,50 = *fünfzig Cent*

a

____

b
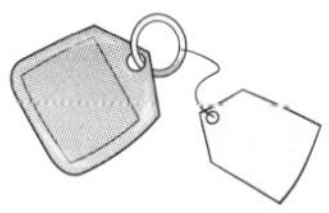
____

c

____

d
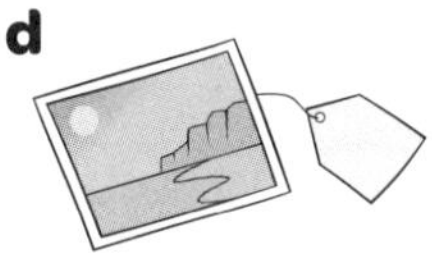
____

e
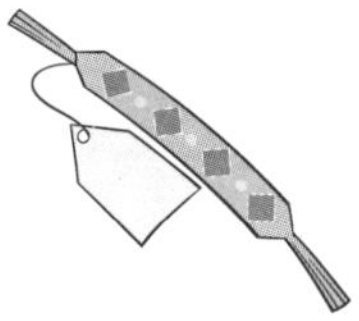
____

f
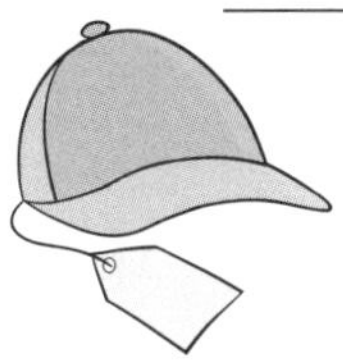
____

g

____

2 From the cloud, choose the correct response to each question to complete the dialogue.

1 Guten Tag! Kann ich dir helfen?

____

____

2 Möchtest du vielleicht einen Kuli?

____

____

3 Welche Farbe? Wir haben blau, rot und auch grün.

____

4 Sonst noch etwas?

____

____

5 Alles zusammen kostet das €15,95.

____

Ja! Ich möchte einen Kuli für meinen Bruder kaufen.

Blau, bitte.

Hallo! Ja, bitte! Ich möchte ein Souvenir kaufen.

Danke. Auf Wiedersehen.

Ja! Ich möchte auch eine Postkarte.

3 Mmm, lecker! (Seiten 102–103)

1 **Write down what you'd say to order the following from the menu.**

1 3×  **2** 2× 

3 1×  **4** 1× 

5 1× 

2×  4× 

Karte

Cola	€2,10
Mineralwasser	€2,60
Bratwurst	€3,40
Pommes	€2,20
Salat	€4,30

Try to use a variety of language. *Ich möchte …* and *Ich hätte gern …* are both ways of saying politely what you'd like.

einmal = one portion of
zweimal/dreimal = two/three portions of
ein Mineralwasser = a mineral water
eine Cola = a cola

1 Ich möchte dreimal Pommes, bitte.
2 ______
3 ______
4 ______
5 ______

2 **The conversation at the snack stand has been jumbled up. Number the lines in the correct order.**

☐ Also, sieben Euro und sechzig Cent. Bitte schön!
☐ **Guten Tag! Was möchten Sie?**
☐ Ja, ich hätte gern ein Mineralwasser.
☐ **Das macht sieben Euro sechzig.**
☐ Guten Tag! Ich möchte einmal Bratwurst mit Pommes und eine Cola, bitte.
☐ **Danke schön. Auf Wiedersehen.**
☐ **Sonst noch etwas?**
☐ Tschüs.

3 **Look at the menu in exercise 1. Reply to the question *Was kostet das?* for each item on the menu. Write the prices in words.**

1 Eine Cola kostet zwei Euro zehn.
2 Ein Mineralwasser ______
3 Einmal Bratwurst ______
4 Einmal Pommes ______
5 Einmal Salat ______

4 In den Sommerferien (Seiten 104–105)

1 Complete the table with the missing verbs and pronouns from the cloud.

ich	
	wirst
	wird

wir	
ihr	
	werden
sie	

werdet *er/sie/es*
Sie *werden*
werde *du*
werden

2 Complete the sentences about summer plans by filling in the gaps.

1 Ich werde segeln . 

2 Ich ________ ________________ . 

3 Wir ________ ________________ . 

4 ________ du ________________ ? 

5 Martin ________ ________________ . 

6 Sonny und Abdiq ________ ________________ . 

im Meer schwimmen
tauchen *wandern*
windsurfen
an den Strand gehen

To say what you will do in the future, use the verb *werden* and an infinitive verb.

3 Read the two texts about what Franzi and Mélodie are going to do in the holidays. Then write 'true' or 'false' next to each statement below.

Die Sommerferien sind da! Das finde ich total super! Ich werde mit meiner Familie nach Ankara in der Türkei fahren. Wir werden zwei Wochen bleiben. Es gibt dort einen fantastischen Marktplatz, wo man tolle Souvenirs kaufen kann. Wir werden auch schwimmen und ins Restaurant gehen. Ich esse sehr gern türkisches Essen!

Franzi aus Worms

Nächste Woche beginnen hier in Hamburg die Sommerferien. Leider werden wir dieses Jahr zu Hause bleiben. In Hamburg gibt es einen sehr großen See und hier kann man schwimmen. Ich möchte auch wandern und werde jeden Tag Rad fahren. Meine Großeltern und Tante wohnen auch in Hamburg. Ich werde sie auch oft in den Sommerferien besuchen.

Mélodie aus Hamburg

besuchen = to visit

1 Franzi is going to stay two weeks in Ankara. ________

2 Ankara is in Switzerland. ________

3 Mélodie is going abroad in the holidays. ________

4 You can swim in the lake in Hamburg. ________

5 The souvenirs at the market in Ankara are awful. ________

6 Mélodie will be visiting relatives in the holidays. ________

1 **Complete the grid with the German words from the cloud to match the English words.**

1 expensive
2 touristy
3 pretty
4 modern
5 great
6 near to
7 to go shopping
8 I would like
9 I will
10 you can
11 very
12 quite
13 always
14 often
15 never

einkaufen gehen
ich möchte
ich werde
immer
in der Nähe von
man kann
modern
schön
nie
oft
sehr
teuer
toll
touristisch
ziemlich

2 **Use words from the cloud in exercise 1 to fill the gaps.**

Düsseldorf ist __________ [great] und ist ____________________ [near to] Köln. Die Königsallee ist sehr beliebt und hier kann man gut ____________________ [go shopping], aber es ist alles hier ____________________ [quite expensive]. ____________________ [You can] in Düsseldorf auch japanisches Essen finden, weil hier viele Japaner wohnen. ____________________ [I'd like] den Rheinturm besuchen, aber das ist sehr ____________________ [touristy]! Nächstes Jahr werde ich Düsseldorf besuchen.

der Rheinturm

beliebt = popular
Japaner = Japanese people

3 **Now use some of the words from exercise 1 and the model text in exercise 2 to write a short text about a town you'd like to visit.**

It is very helpful to use a model text for your writing. Adapt the text in exercise 2 and make sure you include:

- 1 future tense verb
- 1 opinion
- 2 linking words
- 1 time phrase
- 1 example of inverted word order
- 1 reference to other people.

1 **Find seven words for foods and drinks in the wordsearch puzzle. Write the words as you find them**

s	B	r	a	t	w	u	r	s	t	d	P	g
T	i	m	u	e	S	o	r	f	n	c	o	a
e	h	S	a	v	a	p	E	i	s	n	m	k
e	n	e	l	f	l	j	i	t	e	s	m	d
M	i	n	e	r	a	l	w	a	s	s	e	r
a	m	f	c	g	t	h	a	b	u	z	s	l

______
______
______
______
______
______
______

2 **Put the letters in the right order to spell five different souvenirs.**

1 das Kerchuselti ______
2 die Pkeosattr ______
3 der erAleufkb ______
4 die seaTs ______
5 die papeK ______

3 **Choose words from exercises 1 and 2 to answer the questions below. You will need to use some other words too in order to make whole sentences.**

1 Was möchtest du trinken?
Ich möchte ______

2 Was möchtest du essen?
Ich möchte ______

3 Was wirst du als Souvenir kaufen?
Als Souvenir ______

4 Was möchte deine Mutter als Souvenir?
Meine Mutter ______

5 Wirst du das Kuscheltier für deinen Bruder kaufen?
Nein. Für meinen Bruder werde ______

6 Was kann man hier trinken?
Hier ______

7 Was essen Sie gern?
Ich esse ______

Wiederholung 2

1 **Write the price of each item in a full sentence.**

1 Der Kuli kostet zwei Euro zwanzig.

2 ______

3 ______

4 ______

5 ______

6 ______

Check the gender of the souvenirs on page 57 if you need to.

2 **Unjumble the sentences and write them correctly.**

Make sure you've placed the verb in second position, and any infinitives at the end.

1 Berlin findet fantastisch Xavier

______

2 Park es Berlin In gibt einen großen

______

3 Stadt möchte in kaufen die gehen und Xavier Souvenirs

______

4 werden sehen Wir Brandenburger das Tor

______

5 Ich Rad am fahren werde Montag

______

3 **Write a short dialogue between a waiter and a customer using the waiter's notes to the right.**

2 x Salat
2 x Cola
1 x Schokoladeneis
1 x Vanilleeis
€26,45

• Guten Tag! Was möchten Sie?

△ ______

Use the conversation in exercise 2 on page 50 as a model for your dialogue.

Grammatik (Pages 112–113)

1 Ollie is an optimist. Translate the sentences into English to find out what he says.

1 Es gibt ein Schloss in York. ______

2 Ich möchte ein Kuscheltier kaufen. ______

3 Wir essen eine Pizza! ______

4 Ich werde eine Tasse und einen Kuli kaufen.

______

5 Ich habe einen Hamburger – ich liebe Hamburger!

______

2 Millie is feeling miserable. Rewrite the sentences from exercise 1 using the correct form of *kein*.

1 Es gibt kein ______

2 ______

3 ______

4 ______

5 ______

Grammatik
einen → keinen
eine → keine
ein → kein

Don't forget to change *ich liebe* to a negative phrase.

3 Complete the verb table with the words from the cloud.

ich	
du	
	möchte

wir	
ihr	
	möchten

Sie
er/sie/es
sie
möchten
möchtest
möchte
möchten
möchtet

Now complete the sentences about what activities these people would like to do. You choose the activities.

Example: Ich möchte Rad fahren.

1 Ich ______

2 Regina ______

3 Du ______

4 Petra und Sally ______

5 Ihr ______

6 Herr Braun, Sie ______

Remember that after the correct form of *möchten*, the infinitive goes at the end!

Jahresbilanz

Record your levels for *Kapitel* 5.

Listening	I have reached Level ______ in **Listening**.
Speaking	I have reached Level ______ in **Speaking**.
Reading	I have reached Level ______ in **Reading**.
Writing	I have reached Level ______ in **Writing**.

Look back through your workbook and note down the level you achieved in each skill by the end of each *Kapitel*.

	Listening	**Speaking**	**Reading**	**Writing**
1 Meine Welt und ich				
2 Familie und Tiere				
3 Freizeit – juhu!				
4 Schule ist klasse!				
5 Gute Reise!				

You now have a record of your progress in German for the whole year.

In der Stadt • In town

Es gibt ...	*There is ... / There are ...*
Es gibt ein/eine/einen ...	*There is/are a ...*
Es gibt kein/keine/keinen ...	*There isn't/aren't ...*
in der Nähe von ...	*near to*
in der Nähe ...	*nearby*
der Bahnhof(¨-e)	*railway station(s)*
der Imbiss(-e)/die Imbissstube(-n)	*snack stand(s)*
die Kegelbahn(-en)	*bowling alley(s)*
das Kino(-s)	*cinema(s)*
die Kirche(-n)	*church(es)*
der Marktplatz(¨-e)	*market square(s)*
der Park(-s)	*park(s)*
das Schloss(¨-er)	*castle(s)*
das Schwimmbad(¨-er)	*swimming pool(s)*
die Eisbahn(-en)	*ice rink(s)*
der Fischmarkt(¨-e)	*fish market(s)*
das Kindertheater(-)	*children's theatre(s)*
der Radweg(-e)	*cycle path(s)*
das Sportzentrum (die Sportzentren)	*sports centre (sports centres)*
der Stadtpark(-s)	*city/town park(s)*
der Wasserpark(-s)	*water park(s)*

Verkaufsgespräch • Sales conversation

Ich gehe einkaufen.	*I am going shopping.*
Ich möchte ...	*I would like ...*
Ich möchte ... kaufen.	*I would like to buy ...*
Haben Sie ...?	*Do you have ...?*
Kann ich dir helfen?	*Can I help you?*
Sonst noch etwas?	*Anything else?*
alles zusammen	*all together*

Souvenirs • Souvenirs

der Aufkleber	*sticker*
das Freundschafts-band	*friendship bracelet*
die Kappe	*(baseball) cap*
der Kuli	*biro*
das Kuscheltier	*cuddly toy*
die Postkarte	*postcard*
der Schlüsselanhänger	*key ring*
die Tasse	*mug/cup*
das Trikot	*(football) shirt*
Wie viel kostet ...?	*How much does ... cost?*
Wie viel kostet das?	*How much does it cost?*
Es kostet €16.	*It costs 16 Euros.*

Snacks und Getränke kaufen • Buying snacks and drinks

die Bratwurst	*fried sausage*
der Hamburger	*hamburger*
die Pizza	*pizza*
die Pommes	*chips*
der Salat	*salad*
das Eis	*ice cream*
die Cola	*cola*
das Mineralwasser	*mineral water*
der Tee	*tea*
das Fleisch	*meat*
der Ketchup	*ketchup*
die Mayo(nnaise)/Majonäse	*mayo(nnaise)*
der Senf	*mustard*
Ich möchte einmal/zweimal/dreimal ...	*I would like one/two/three ...*
Ich hätte gern ...	*I would like ...*
Das macht €8.	*That's €8.*
Ich esse ... gern.	*I like eating ... .*
Ich trinke ... gern.	*I like drinking ... .*

Wörter

In den Sommerferien • During the summer holidays

Was wirst du machen?	*What will you do?*
Ich werde ...	*I will ...*
Wir werden ...	*We will ...*
klettern	*climb*
im Meer schwimmen	*swim in the sea*
rodeln	*toboggan*
im See baden	*bathe in the lake*
segeln	*sail*
an den Strand gehen	*go to the beach*
tauchen	*dive*
wandern	*hike*
windsurfen	*windsurf*
Was kann man dort machen?	*What can you do there?*
Man kann ... besuchen.	*'One'/People/ You can visit ...*
Die Stadt ist bekannt für ...	*The town is well known for ...*
Ich werde (eine Woche) bleiben.	*I will stay (for a week).*

Oft benutzte Wörter • High-frequency words

am Montag	*on Monday*
am Dienstag	*on Tuesday*
am Mittwoch	*on Wednesday*
am Donnerstag	*on Thursday*
am Freitag	*on Friday*
am Wochenende	*at the weekend*
sehr	*very*
nicht sehr	*not very*
ziemlich	*quite*
immer	*always*
nicht immer	*not always*
oft	*often*
nicht oft	*not often*
nie	*never*
alles	*everything*
dort	*there*
teuer	*expensive*

Level descriptors

Listening

Level 1	I can understand some familiar spoken words and phrases.
Level 2	I can understand a range of familiar spoken phrases.
Level 3	I can understand the main points of short spoken passages and note people's answers to questions.
Level 4	I can understand the main points of spoken passages and some of the detail.
Level 5	I can understand the main points and opinions in spoken passages about different topics. I can recognise if people are speaking about the future **OR** the past as well as the present.

Speaking

Level 1	I can say single words and short phrases.
Level 2	I can answer simple questions and use set phrases.
Level 3	I can ask questions and use short phrases to answer questions about myself.
Level 4	I can take part in conversations. I can express my opinions. I can use grammar to change phrases to say something new.
Level 5	I can give short talks, in which I express my opinions. I can take part in conversations giving information, opinions and reasons. I can speak about the future **OR** the past as well as the present.

Level descriptors

Reading

Level 1	I can understand familiar words and phrases.
Level 2	I can understand familiar phrases. I can read aloud familiar words and phrases. I can use a vocabulary list to check meanings.
Level 3	I can understand the main points and people's answers to questions in short written texts.
Level 4	I can understand the main points in short texts and some of the detail. Sometimes I can work out the meaning of new words.
Level 5	I can understand the main points and opinions in texts about different topics. I can recognise if the texts are about the future **OR** the past as well as the present.

Writing

Level 1	I can write or copy single words correctly.
Level 2	I can copy short sentences correctly and write some words from memory.
Level 3	I can answer questions about myself. I can write short phrases from memory. I can write short sentences with help.
Level 4	I can write short texts on familiar topics. I can use grammar to change phrases to write something new.
Level 5	I can write short texts on a range of familiar topics. I can write about the future **OR** the past as well as the present.

Notes

Notes

Published by Pearson Education Limited, Edinburgh Gate, Harlow, Essex, CM20 2JE.

www.pearsonschoolsandfecolleges.co.uk

Edited by Melanie Birdsall
Designed by Kamae Design

Illustrated by Caron at KJA Artists and Lisa Hunt

First published 2013

19
10 9

British Library Cataloguing in Publication Data
A catalogue record for this book is available from the British Library

ISBN 978 1 447 94653 3

Printed in Malaysia (CTP-PJB)

Acknowledgements

We would like to thank Melissa Weir, Angelika Libera, Janet Soame and Frances Reynolds for their invaluable help in the development of this course.

Every effort has been made to contact copyright holders of material reproduced in this book. Any omissions will be rectified in subsequent printings if notice is given to the publishers.

www.pearsonschools.co.uk
myorders@pearson.com
T 0845 630 33 33
F 0845 630 77 77

ISBN 978-1-4479-4653-3

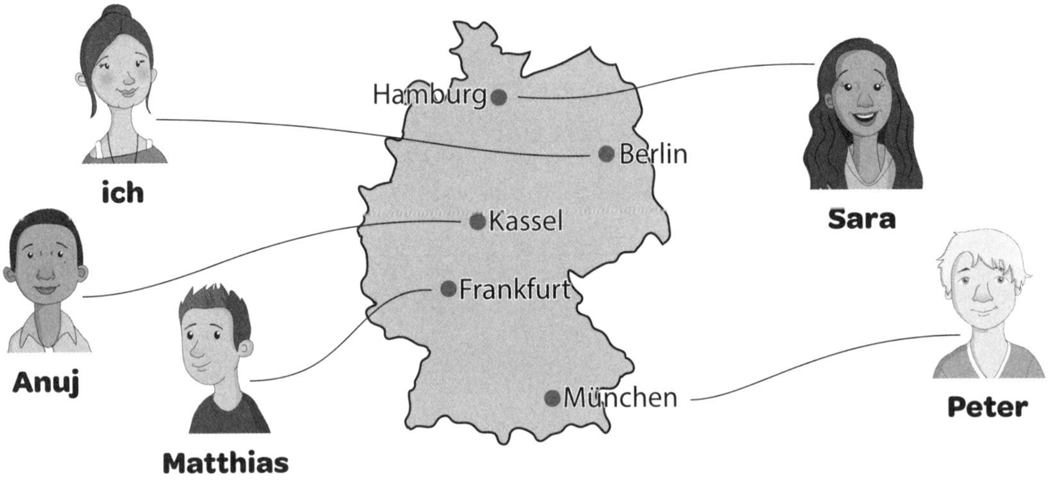

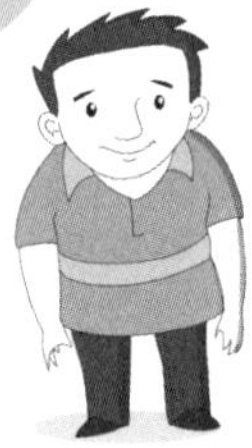

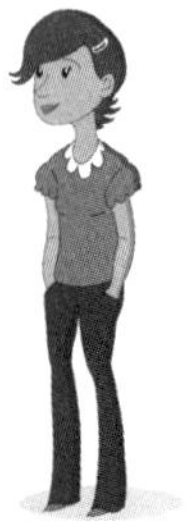

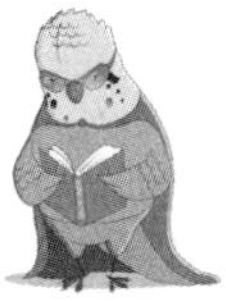 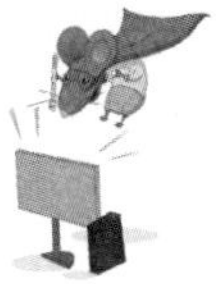 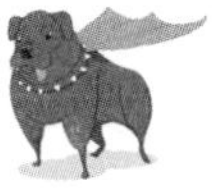 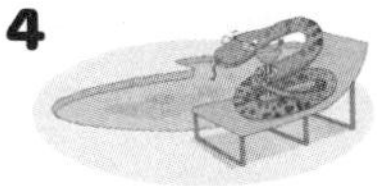 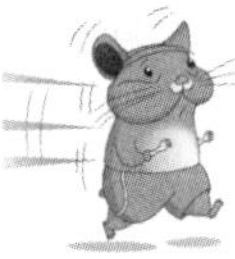 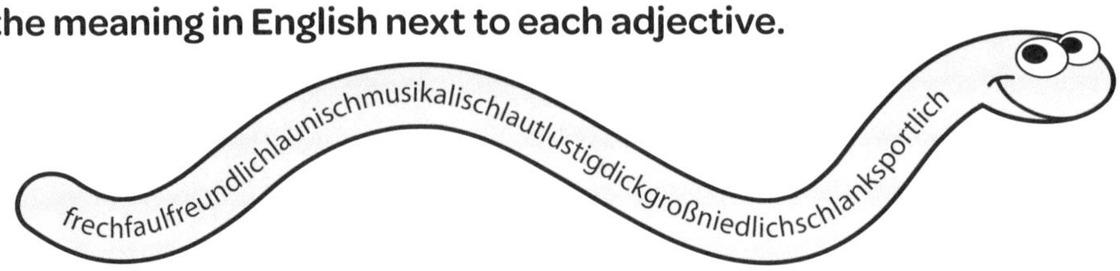

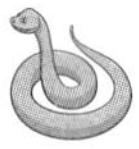 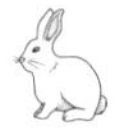 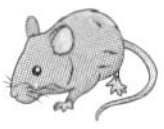 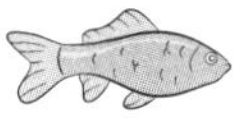 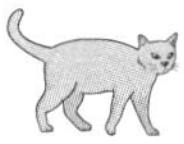 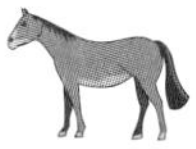 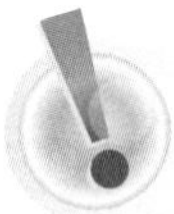
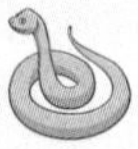 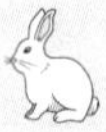 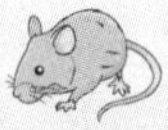 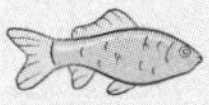 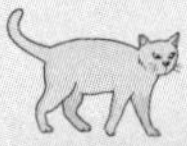 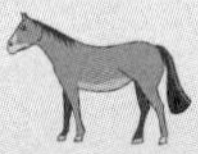  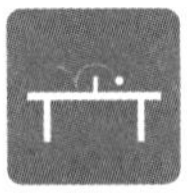   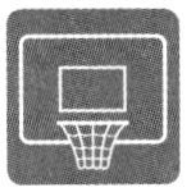  

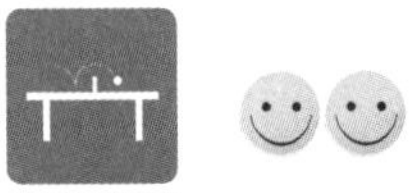 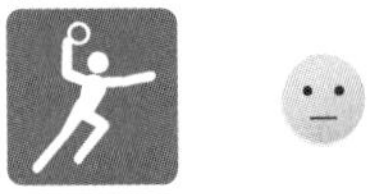  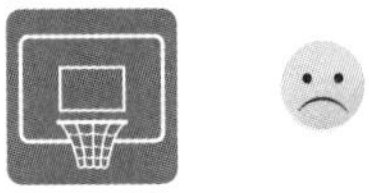 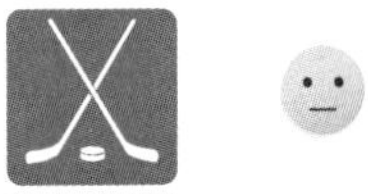   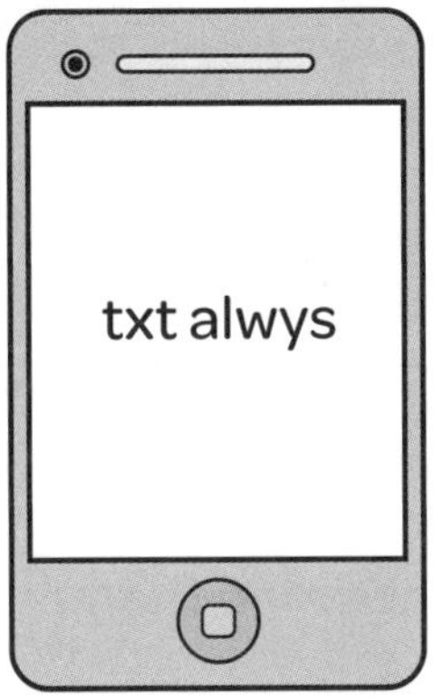

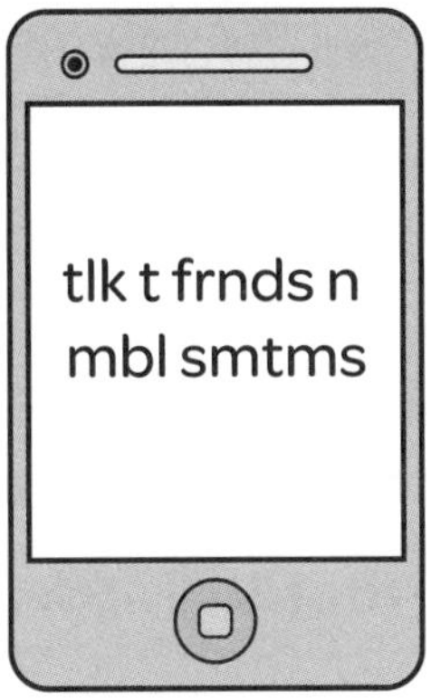

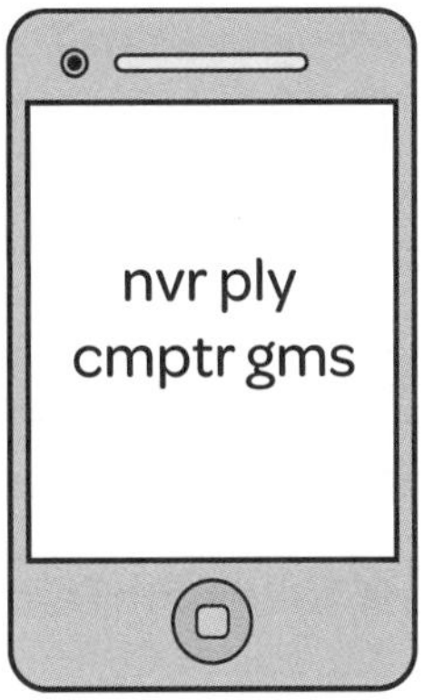

Brieffreunde (Seiten 64–65)

1 Complete the email with the phrases from the cloud. Don't forget the punctuation!

1 ______________________

Danke 2 ______________________

3 ______________________ Es geht mir gut.

Ich habe viele Hobbys! Ich finde Sport super und ich spiele sehr gern Tischtennis, weil es toll ist! Ich gehe am Wochenende in den Park und spiele immer Fußball mit meinen Freunden. Musik finde ich toll. Ich höre jeden Tag Musik auf meinem iPhone und ich spiele Trompete. Meine Freundin Nerida spielt Keyboard in meiner Band. Manchmal essen wir zusammen einen Hamburger oder eine Pizza.

4 ______________________

5 ______________________

Andrea

für deine E-Mail!
Lieber Stephen,
Liebe Grüße
Wie geht's?
Schreib bald!

zusammen = together
Schreib bald! = Write soon!

2 Find the following features in the email above and underline them.

- 2 opinions
- 3 connecting words
- 2 time phrases
- 1 reference to another person
- 1 example of inverted word order (verb second after a time phrase)

Picking out features from a model text and adapting them will help you to add variety to your writing.

3 Complete the email below with the type of word indicated by the number.

Hallo Susi!

Ich __heiße__ (1) Mona und ich komme aus Schottland. Ich ______________ (1) sehr gern Badminton, aber mein Lieblingssport ist ______________ (2). Ich ______________ (1) Badminton super. Ich lese auch ______________ (5) Magazine und ______________ (5) Blogs. Wasserball ______________ (4) Eishockey spiele ich nicht gern. Eishockey ist ______________. (3) Mein Freund Julian ______________ (1) auch gern ______________ (2), ______________ (4) nicht so gern Gitarre.

Deine Mona

Look at the model text in exercise 1 but try to use different words to fill the gaps.

(1) verb
(2) noun
(3) adjective
(4) connecting word
(5) frequency expression

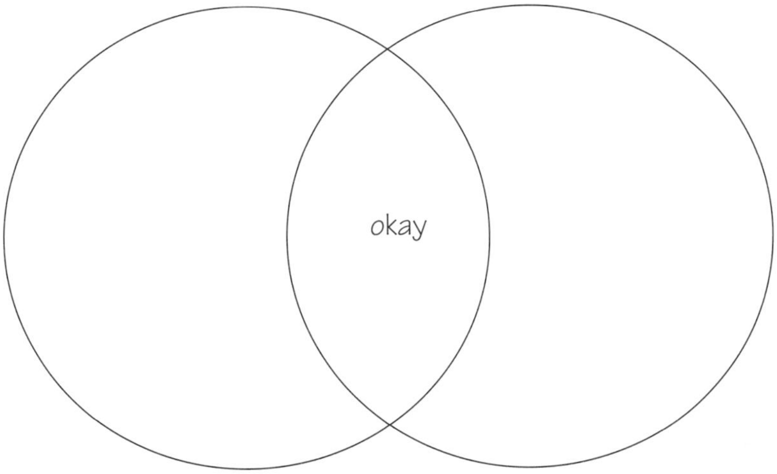

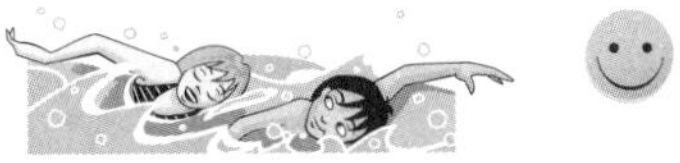

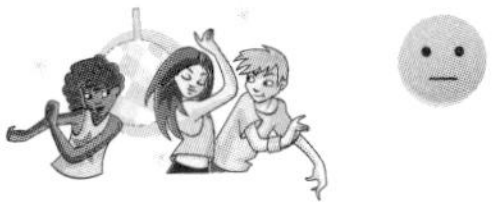

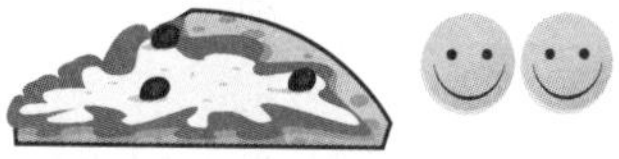

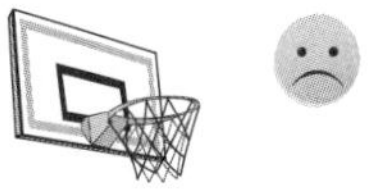

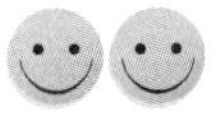 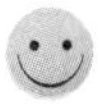   # 6 Writing Skills
Willkommen! (Seiten 108–109)

1 Complete the grid with the German words from the cloud to match the English words.

1 expensive
2 touristy
3 pretty
4 modern
5 great
6 near to
7 to go shopping
8 I would like
9 I will
10 you can
11 very
12 quite
13 always
14 often
15 never

einkaufen gehen
ich möchte
ich werde
immer
in der Nähe von
man kann
modern
schön
nie
oft
sehr
teuer
toll
touristisch
ziemlich

2 Use words from the cloud in exercise 1 to fill the gaps.

Düsseldorf ist __________ [great] und ist __________________ [near to] Köln. Die Königsallee ist sehr beliebt und hier kann man gut ______________________ [go shopping], aber es ist alles hier ______________________ [quite expensive].

__________________ [You can] in Düsseldorf auch japanisches Essen finden, weil hier viele Japaner wohnen.

______________________ [I'd like] den Rheinturm besuchen, aber das ist sehr __________________ [touristy]!

Nächstes Jahr werde ich Düsseldorf besuchen.

der Rheinturm

beliebt = popular
Japaner = Japanese people

3 Now use some of the words from exercise 1 and the model text in exercise 2 to write a short text about a town you'd like to visit.

It is very helpful to use a model text for your writing. Adapt the text in exercise 2 and make sure you include:

- 1 future tense verb
- 1 opinion
- 2 linking words
- 1 time phrase
- 1 example of inverted word order
- 1 reference to other people.

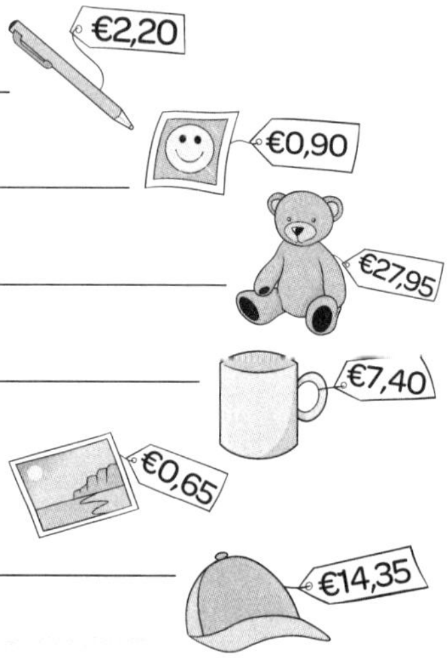

Stimmt! 1

Übungsheft A

Malcolm Pacey

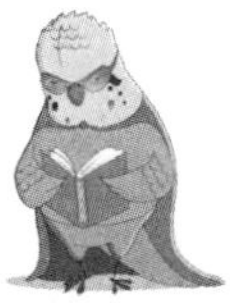 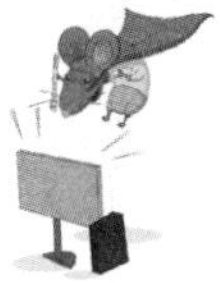 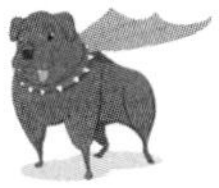 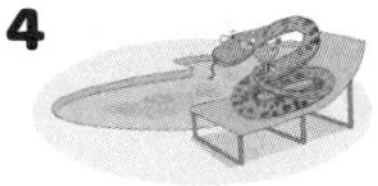 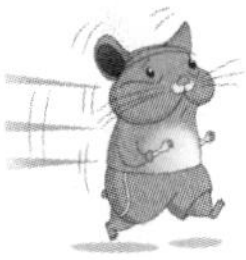 # 4 Die Farben der Welt (Seiten 36–37)

1 Complete the grid with the German words for the colours. Reveal the code word using the letters in the shaded boxes. It is a noun, so remember the capital letter!

Grid	Clue
1	1 red
2	2 orange
3	3 green
4	4 blue
5	5 black
6	6 grey
7	7 white
8	8 purple
9	9 pink
10	10 brown

Markus hat hellblaue _ _ _ _ _ _.

2 Complete the sentences with the correct form of the verb *haben* and the colour.

When describing hair and eyes, you add an 'e' to the colours.

Grammatik

ich habe	wir haben
du hast	ihr habt
er/sie hat	sie/Sie haben

1 Ich __________ kurze __________ Haare.

2 Mein Bruder __________ kurze __________ Haare und __________ Augen.

3 Meine Schwester __________ mittellange __________ Haare und __________ Augen.

4 Mein Vater __________ lange __________ Haare.

5 Meine Mutter __________ kurze __________ Haare und hell __________ Augen.

6 Meine Großeltern __________ __________ Haare und __________ Augen.

5 Alles Gute! (Seiten 38–39)

1 Write the correct date in words next to each calendar page.

1 08.05. am achten Mai
2 19.04. ______
3 07.09. ______
4 01.06. ______
5 03.02. ______
6 22.12. ______
7 29.11. ______

am dritten Februar
am neunzehnten April
~~am achten Mai~~
am ersten Juni
am siebten September
am neunundzwanzigsten November
am zweiundzwanzigsten Dezember

2 Read the profiles and the statements below. Write 'true' or 'false' next to each statement.

Ich heiße Tim und ich wohne in Watford. Ich habe am dreiundzwanzigsten April Geburtstag. Mein Bruder Matthias hat auch im April Geburtstag, aber am dritten.

Hallo, hier ist Anna! Ich habe am vierten Juli Geburtstag. Das ist im Sommer – super! Meine Schwester Adele wohnt in Hamburg. Sie hat am 24. Dezember Geburtstag. Das findet sie nervig.

1 Tim and Matthias share the same birthday. ______
2 Adele is 24 years old. ______
3 Adele doesn't like her birthday. ______
4 Matthias has his birthday before Tim. ______
5 Anna's birthday is on 14 July. ______
6 Anna likes her summer birthday. ______

3 Write a short profile about yourself. Use the profiles in exercise 2 as models.

______
______
______

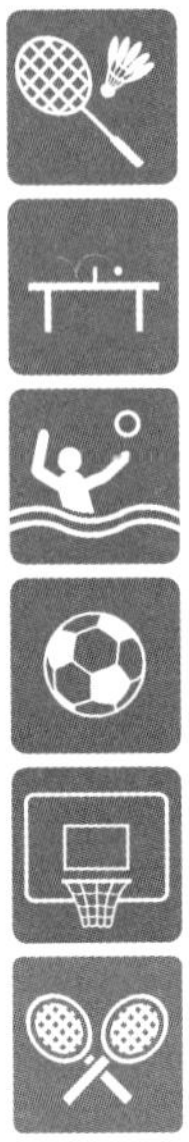

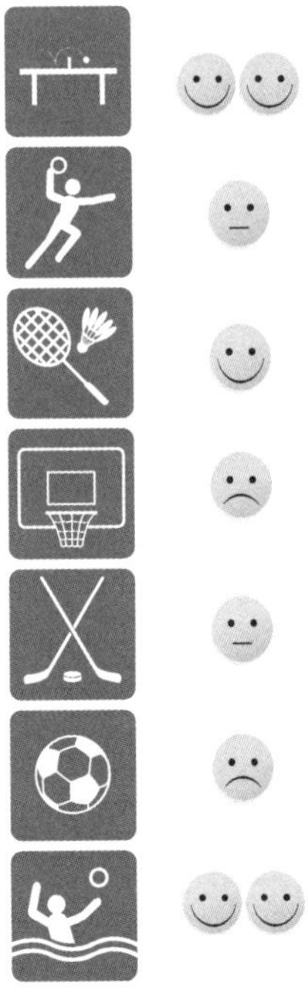

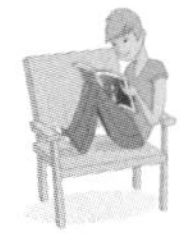 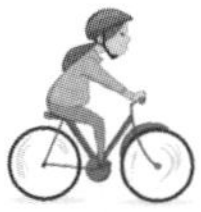 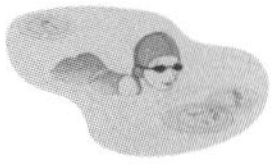 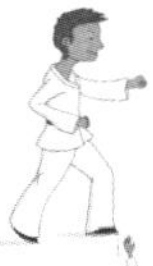 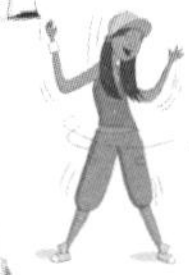 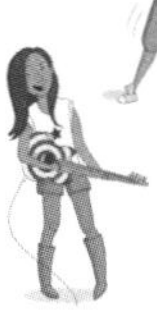 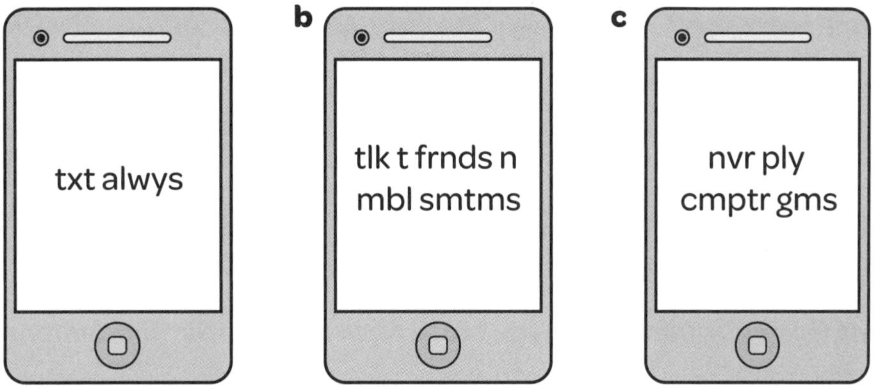

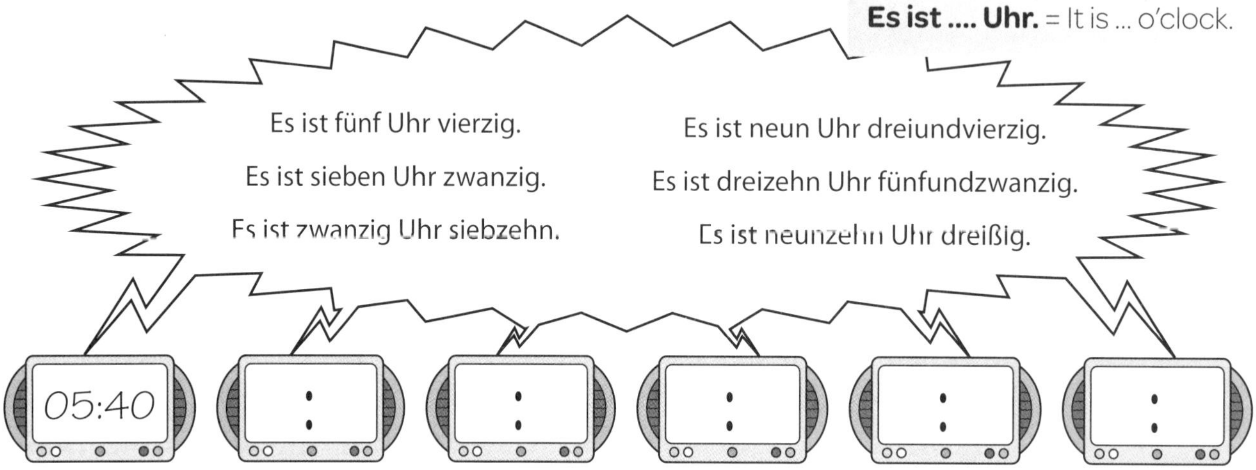

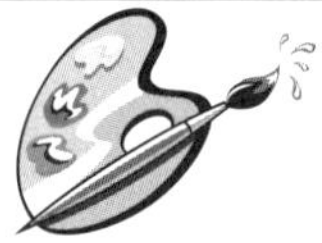 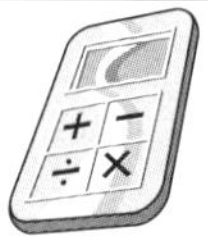 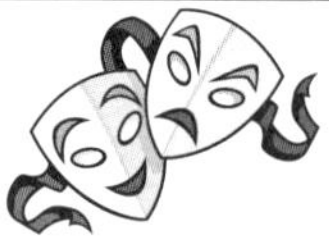 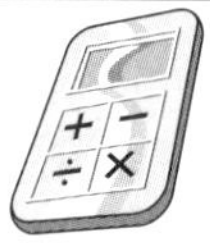 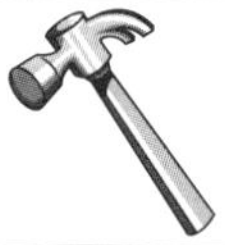 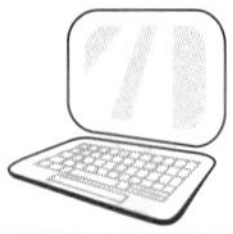 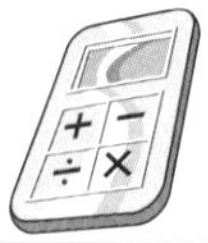 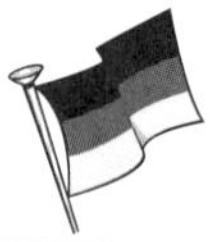 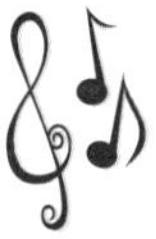 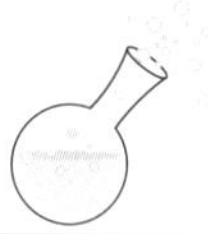 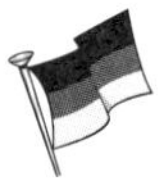 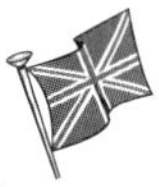 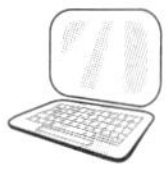 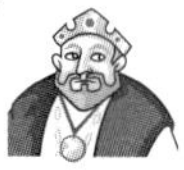 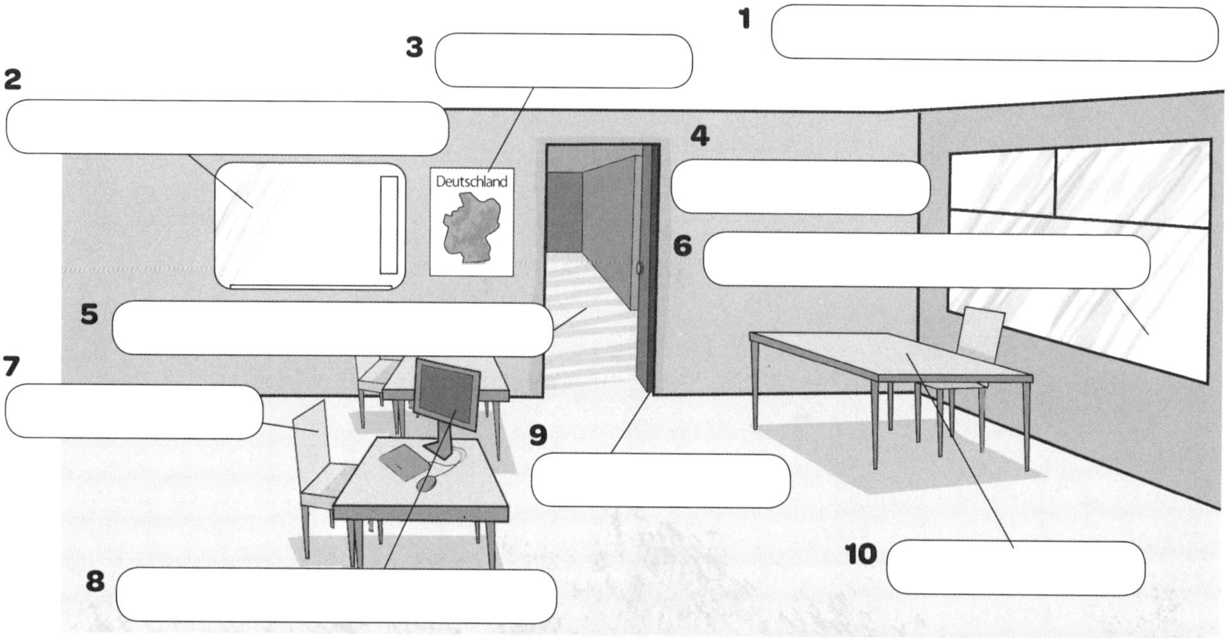

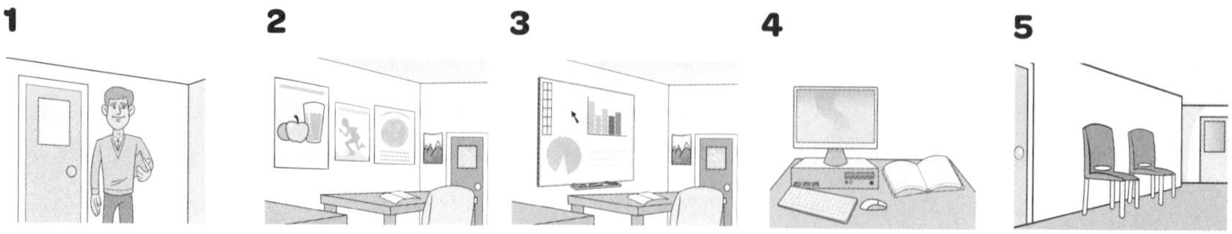

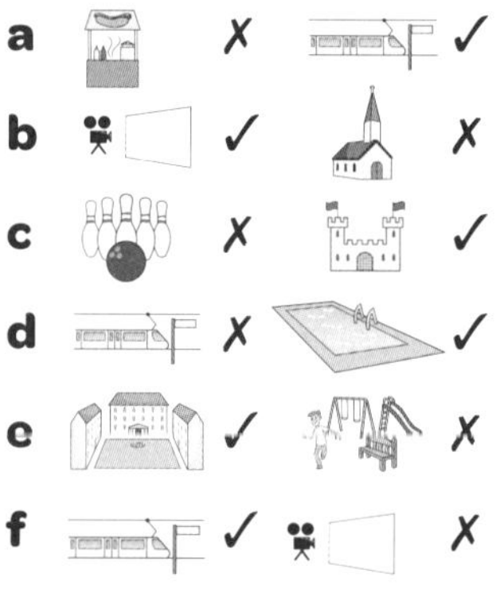

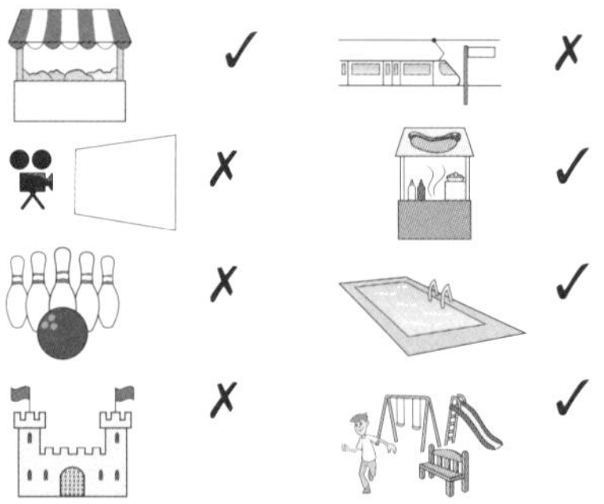

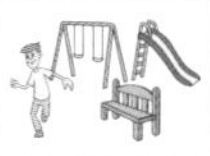 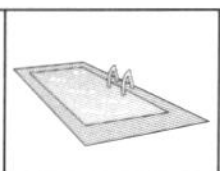 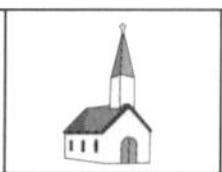 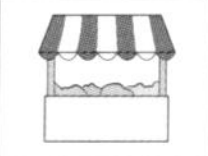  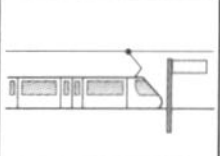 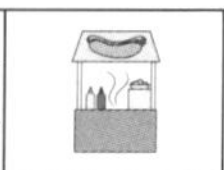 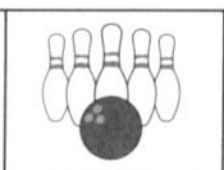  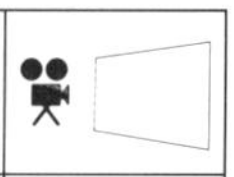 # Stimmt! 1

Übungsheft A

Malcolm Pacey

ALWAYS LEARNING

PEARSON

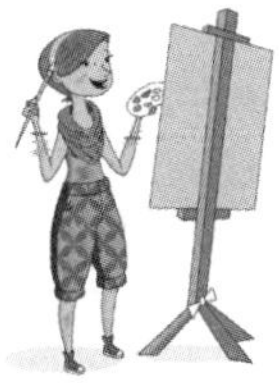 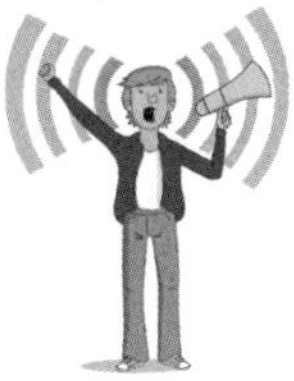 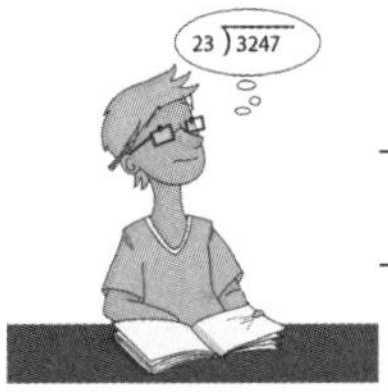

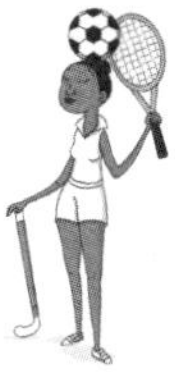 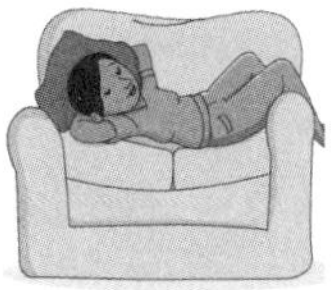 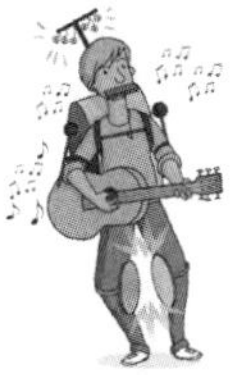 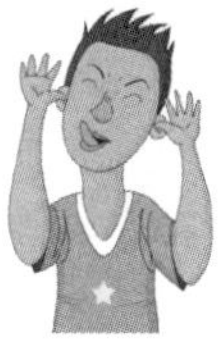 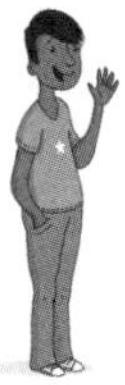 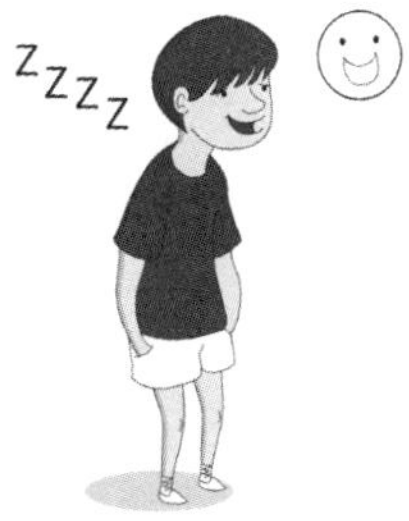

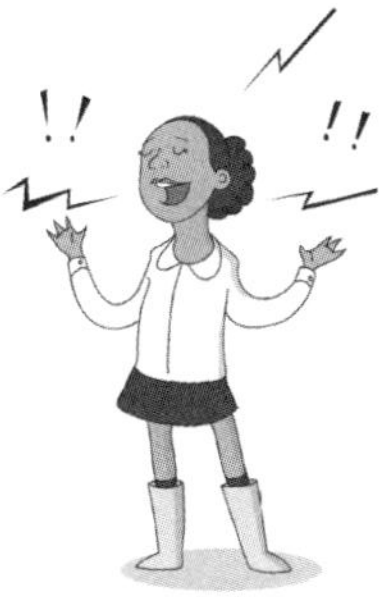

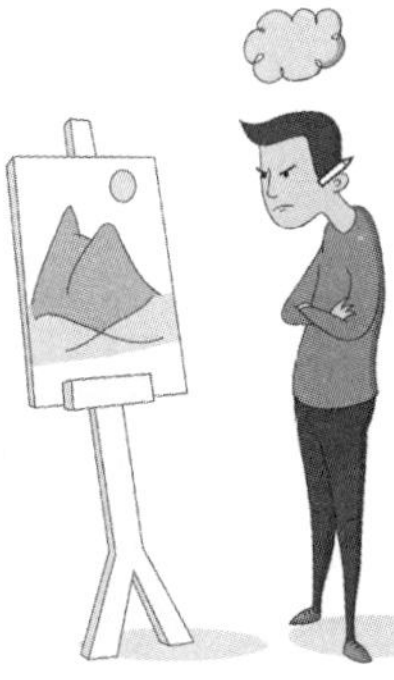

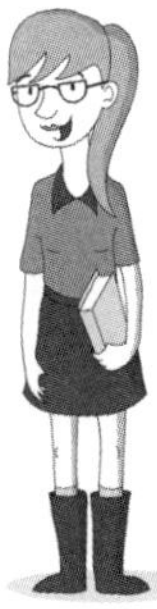

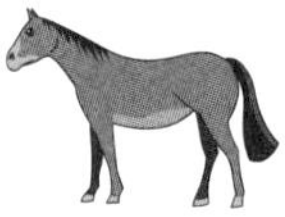

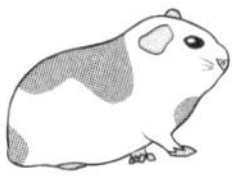

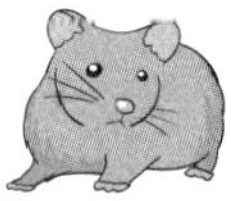

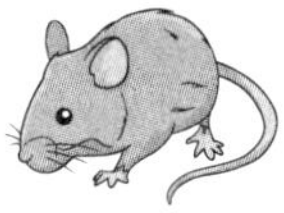

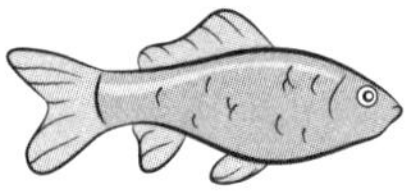

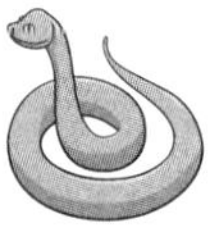

Wiederholung 2

1 Write the house numbers as words.

Karl-Liebknecht-Straße 28 *achtund* ______________

Grünewaldstraße 46 ______________

Prinzstraße 67 ______________

Willy-Brandt-Straße 73 ______________

Neumannstraße 89 ______________

2 Number the highlighted ants with the correct ordinal number. Use the tip box to remind you of how ordinal numbers are formed.

1st = erste 2nd = zweite 3rd = dritte 8th = achte
19th = neunzehnte 20th = zwanzigste

die Ameise = ant

die erste Ameise ______________

1st **5th** **18th** **25th**

3rd **10th** **21st**

3 Use the code to write the words in German.

A	B	C	D	E	F	G	H	I	J	K	L	M	N	O
9	15	10	11	26	2	25	22	14	6	21	5	20	17	27

P	Q	R	S	T	U	V	W	X	Y	Z	Ä	Ö	Ü	ß
7	30	13	8	1	29	19	16	4	23	28	24	18	12	3

a 15 / 5 / 9 / 29 / 26 ______________

b 8 / 10 / 22 / 16 / 9 / 13 / 28 / 26 ______________

c 20 / 14 / 1 / 1 / 26 / 5 / 5 / 9 / 17 / 25 / 26 ______________

d 15 / 13 / 9 / 29 / 17 / 26 ______________

e 21 / 29 / 13 / 28 / 26 ______________

Use some of the decoded words to fill the gaps.

1 Marieke hat ______________ Augen.

2 Hast du ______________?

3 Sie hat ______________ und ______________.

 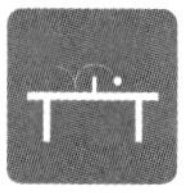   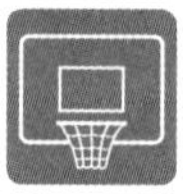  

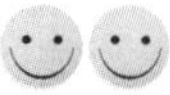

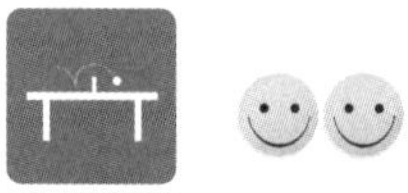 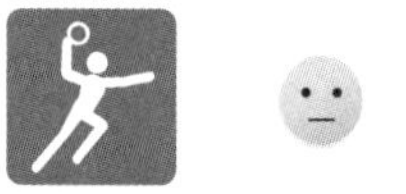 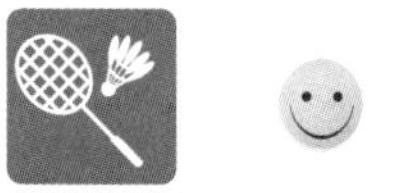 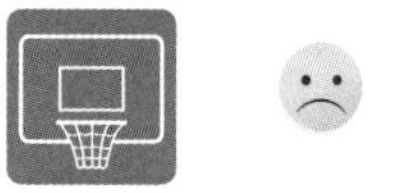 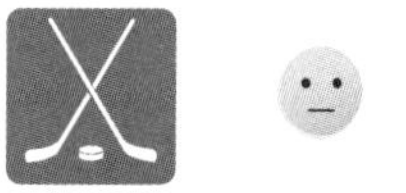 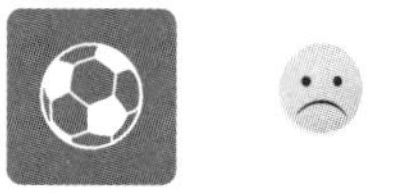 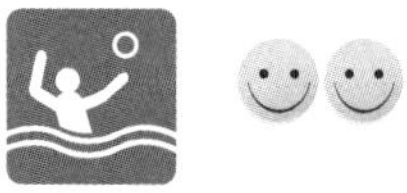 # 4 Im Klassenzimmer (Seiten 82–83)

1 **Use the words in the cloud to label the items in the classroom.**

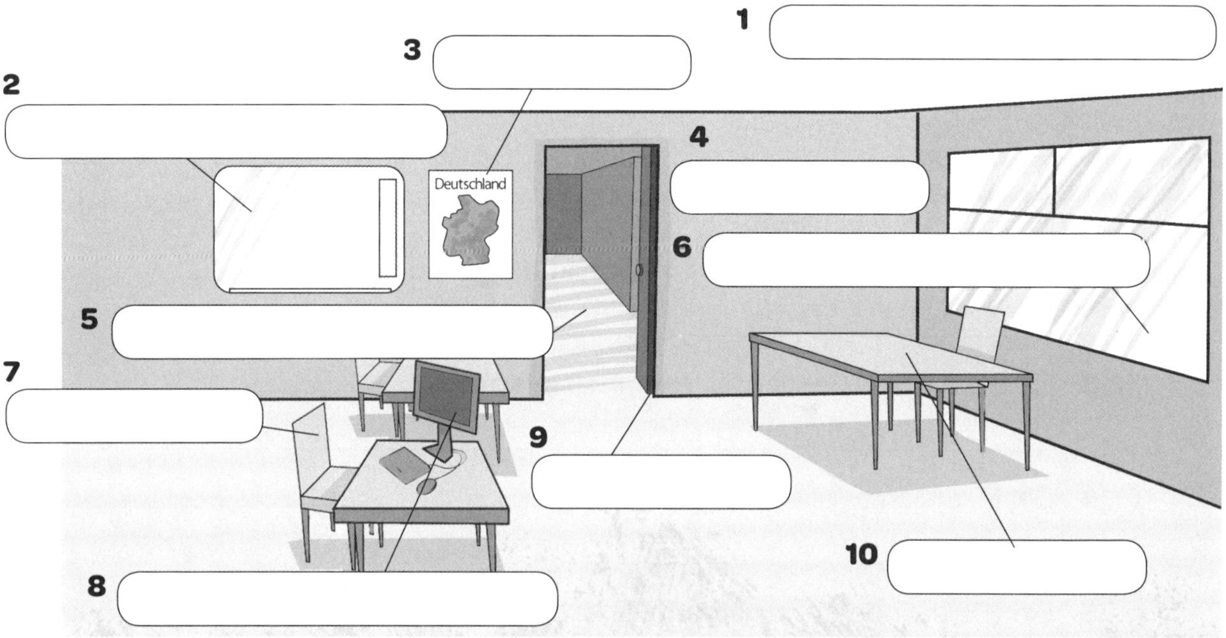

das Klassenzimmer *der Computer* *das Fenster* *der Korridor* *das Poster*
der Stuhl *der Tisch* *die Tür* *die Wand* *das Whiteboard*

2 **Draw lines to match each German phrase with the correct English meaning.**

1 neben dem Computer
2 im Klassenzimmer
3 an der Wand
4 neben der Tür
5 im Korridor

a on the wall
b next to the computer
c in the corridor
d in the classroom
e next to the door

3 **Use the phrases in exercise 2 to help you answer the questions.**

1 
2 
3 
4 
5 

1 Wo ist Herr Peters? Herr Peters ist ____________________

2 Wo sind die Poster? ____________________

3 Wo ist das Whiteboard? ____________________

4 Wo ist das Buch? ____________________

5 Wo sind die Stühle? ____________________

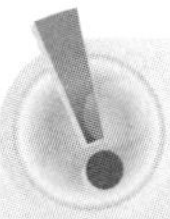

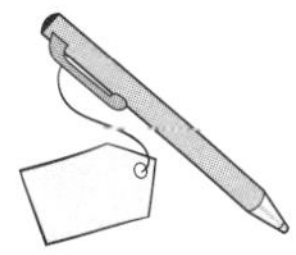
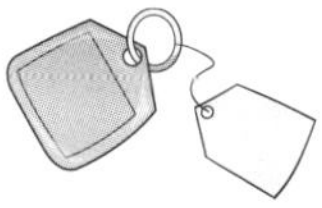
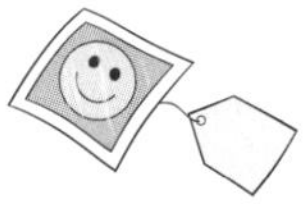
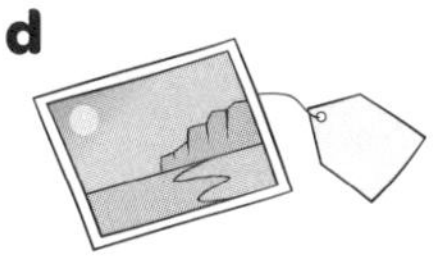
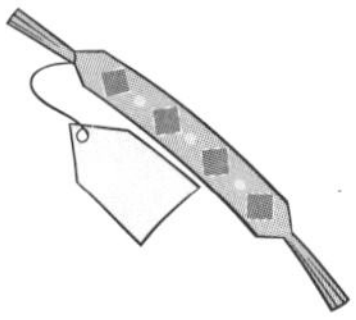
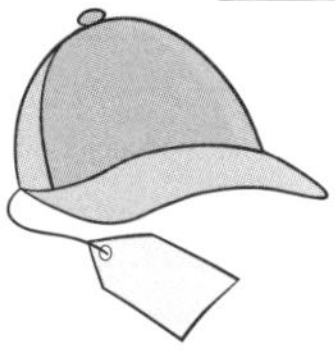
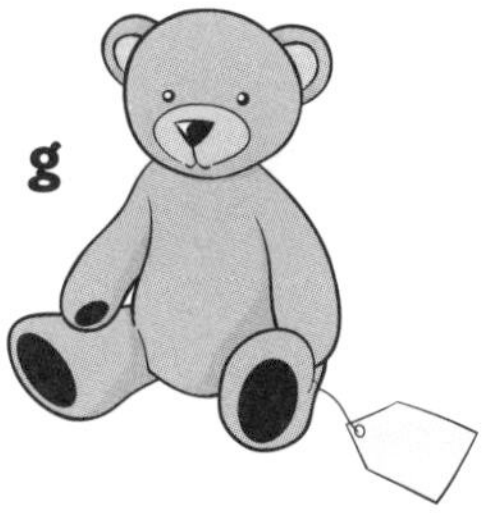
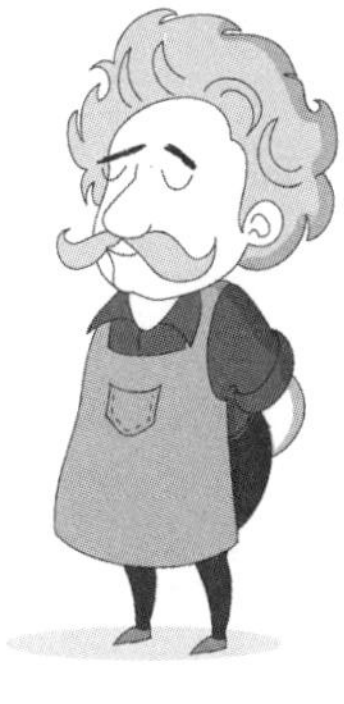

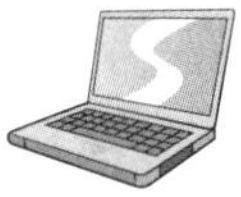 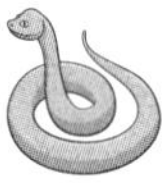 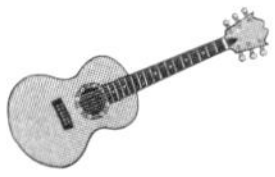 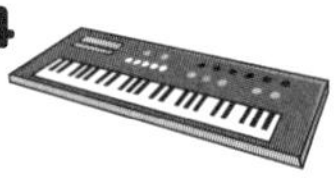 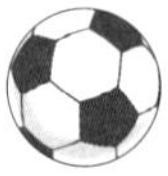 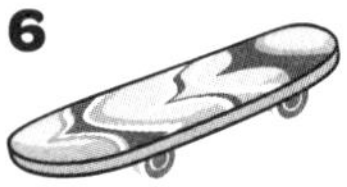 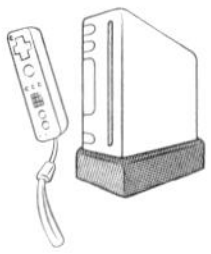 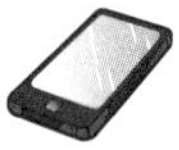 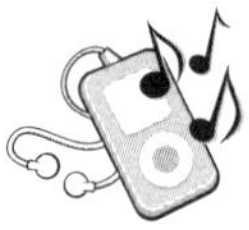 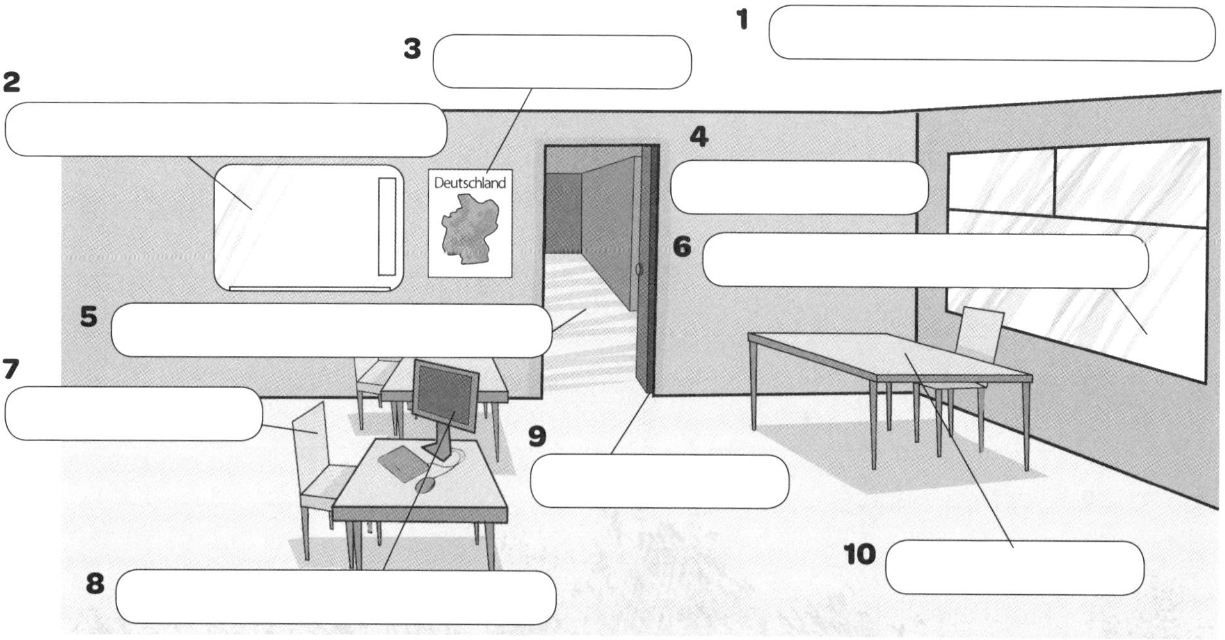

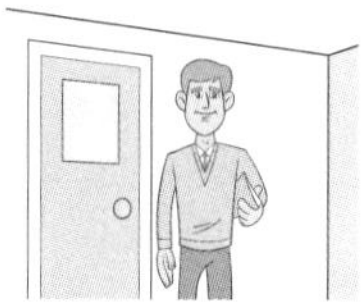

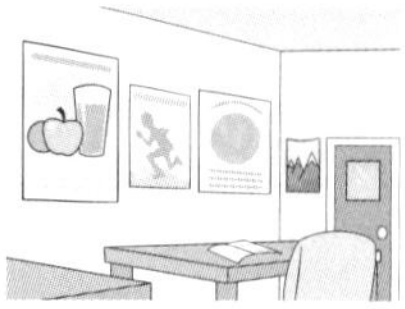

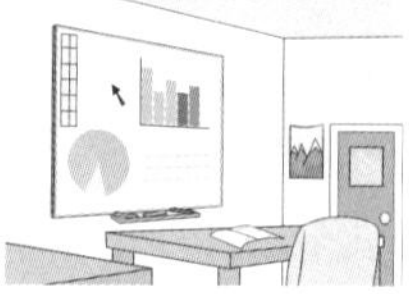

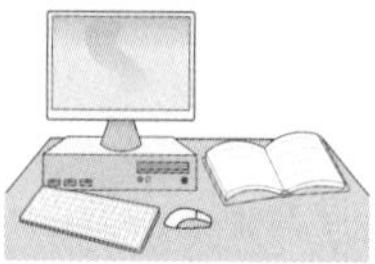

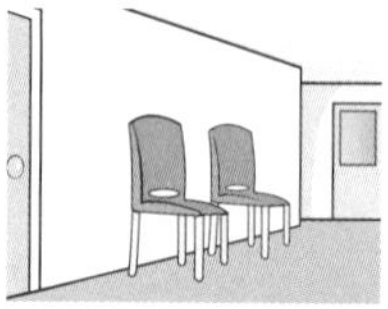

Stimmt! 1

Übungsheft A

Malcolm Pacey

PEARSON

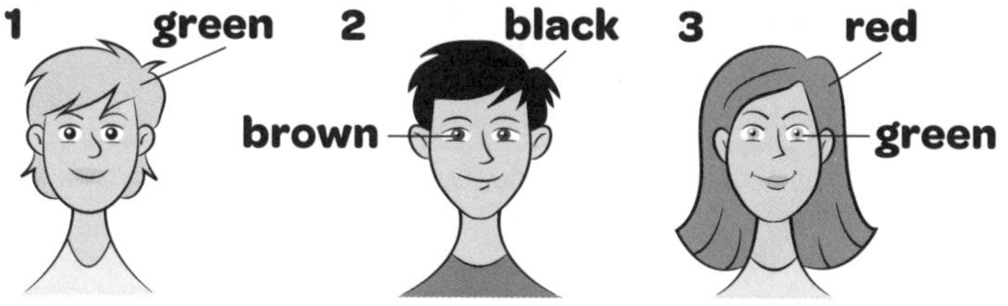

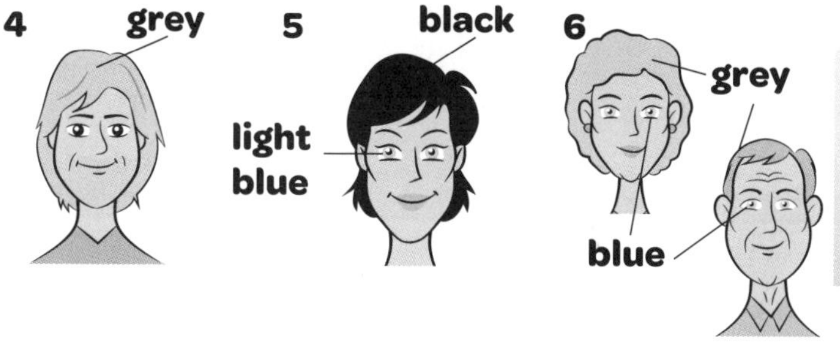

 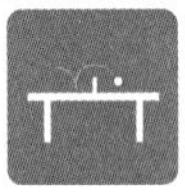   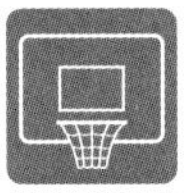  

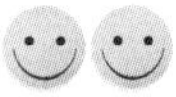

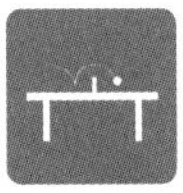 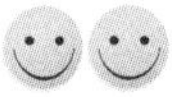 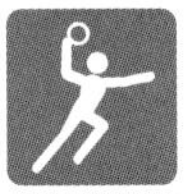   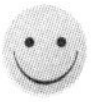 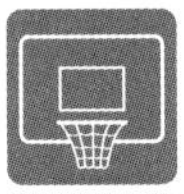  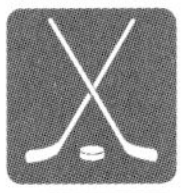 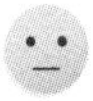    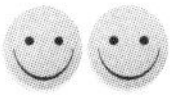 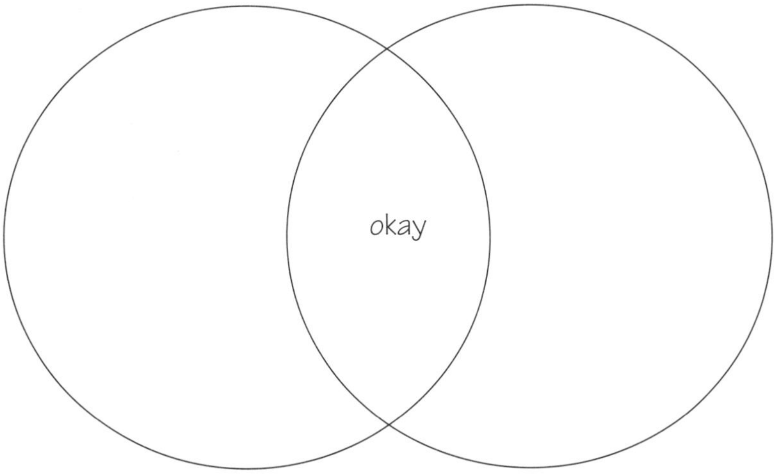

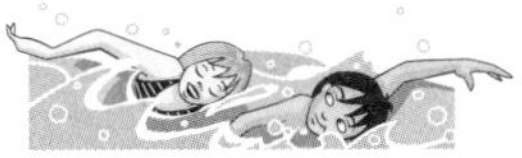 

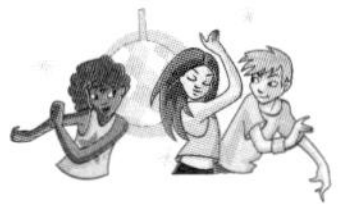 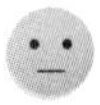

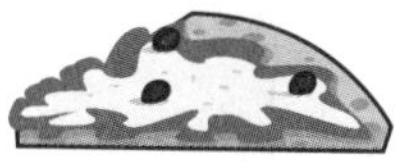 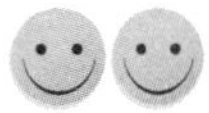

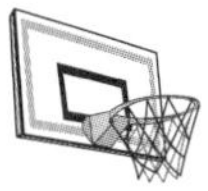 

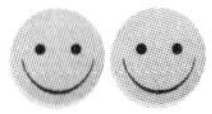  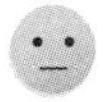  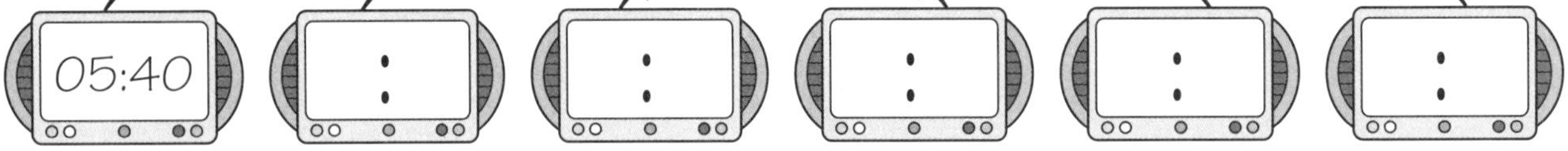

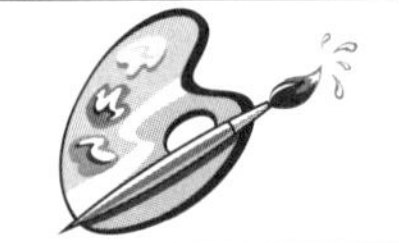 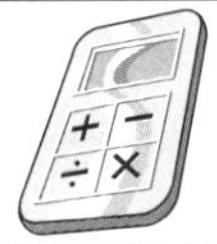 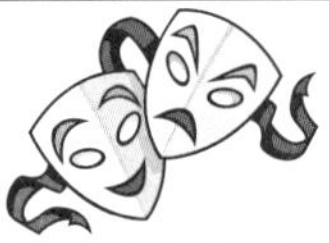 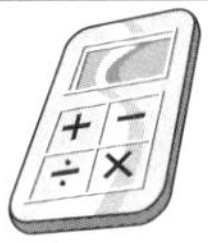 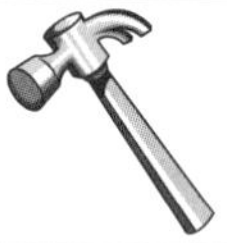 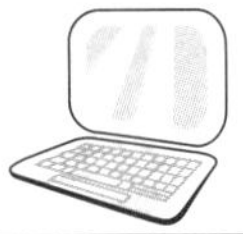 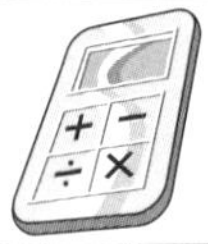 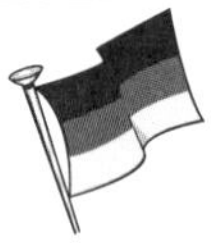 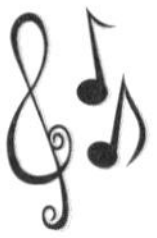 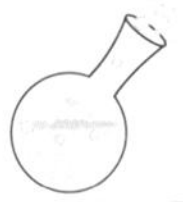 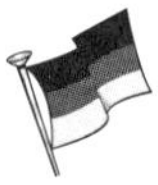  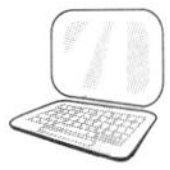 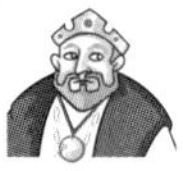 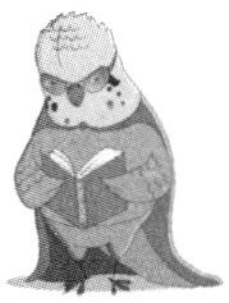 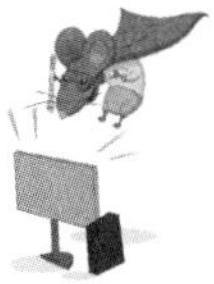 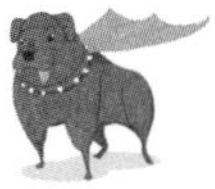 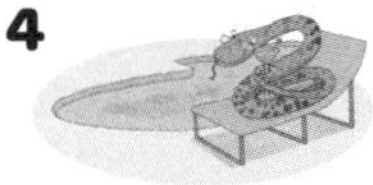 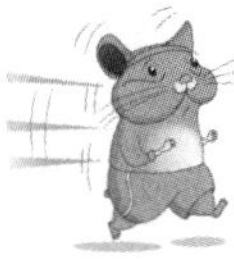 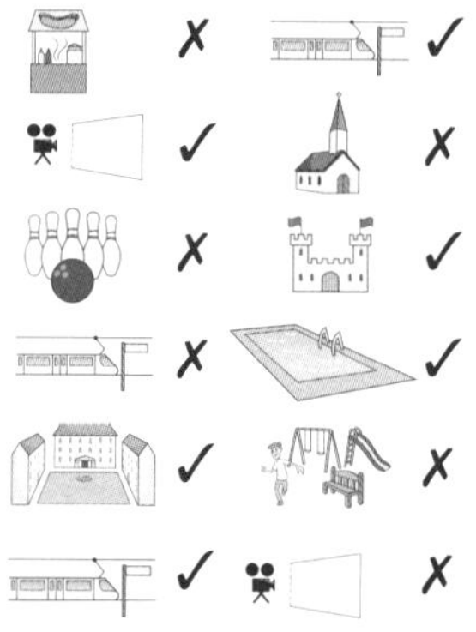

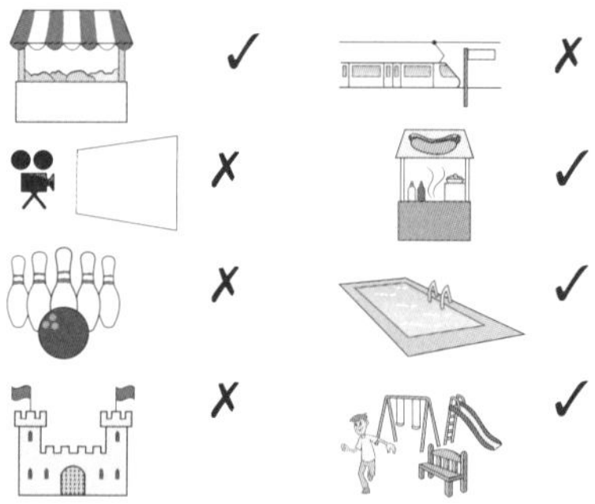

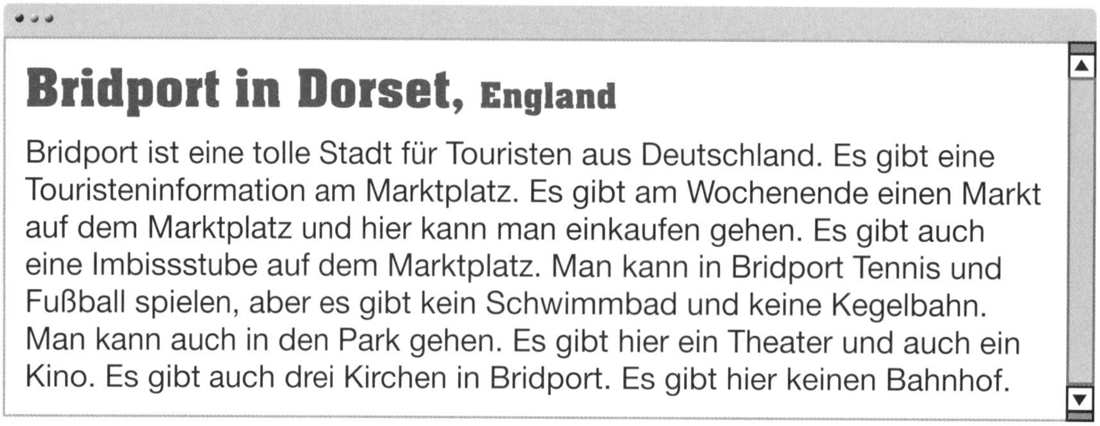

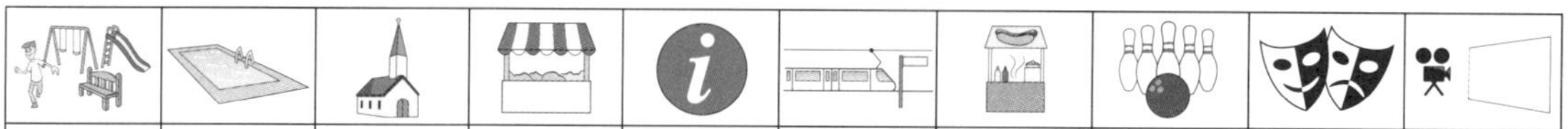

Stimmt! 1

Übungsheft A

Malcolm Pacey

ALWAYS LEARNING

PEARSON

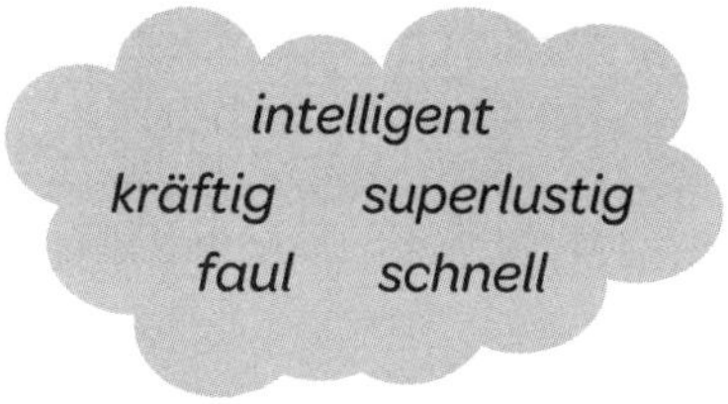

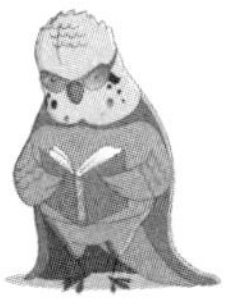 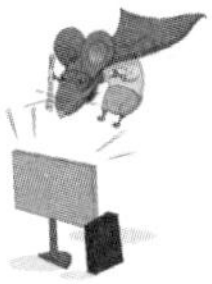 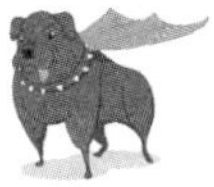 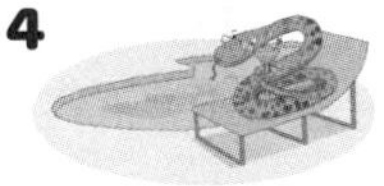 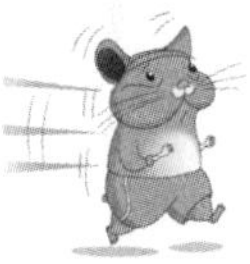